Jesus and Mary - Husband and Wife

Who Were They and What Was Their Relationship?

By Joseph Lumpkin

Joseph Lumpkin

Jesus and Mary - Husband and Wife

Who Were They and What Was Their Relationship

By Joseph Lumpkin

Copyright © 2012

All rights reserved.

Fifth Estate Publisher

2795 County Hwy 57

Blountsville, AL 35031

First Edition

Cover Designed by An Quigley

Printed on acid-free paper

Library of Congress Control No: 2012954177

ISBN: 9781936533312

Fifth Estate, 2012

Joseph Lumpkin

Table of Contents

Joseph Lumpkin

Introduction

Who was Jesus of Nazareth? Do we know what he looked like? What did his followers really think about him? What was being taught about him to those who came into the fold soon after his death? Who was Mary of Magdala? Was she some helpless waif or was she a pivotal and driving force in the life of Jesus? Were Jesus and Mary husband and wife?

We will attempt to present evidence that may shed light on these questions. In an attempt to keep all evidence within context most of the sources quoted will be present to the reader intact in the back of the book. Some of the evidence has been in the hands of church officials and scholars for many years. Some evidence has come to light only in the last few months. All of the evidence has been rejected by the church as unreliable and therefore counted as no evidence at all. Yet, when line upon line and precept upon precept build toward a point it is difficult to continue to reject what has become a body of evidence. However, even if one does say there is no evidence Jesus and Mary were married, the absence of evidence is not the evidence of absence.

*"Absence of evidence is **not** evidence of absence!"*
-- Carl Sagan, Astronomer

This thought provoking quote can be found on page 213 of Carl Sagan's book, "The Demon-Haunted World—Science as a Candle in the Dark". His amazing mind was exploring the false argument used by ancient religious scholars called "*argumentum ad ignorantiam* ("appeal to ignorance"). The argument asserts "something must be true because it cannot be proven to be false".

Sagan's statement may be too broad and may border on its own exaggeration, likely in an attempt to contrast. Attempting to show clearly the lack of logic in "*argumentum ad ignorantiam* he may have fallen into a pit of his own. It is better said that **absence of evidence is not *proof* of absence.**

Argument from ignorance is a fallacy in informal logic. It asserts that a proposition is true because it has not yet been proven false. This sets up a binary choice and excludes a third option, which is that there is insufficient investigation and therefore insufficient information to prove the proposition satisfactorily to be either true or false and may actually be some place in the middle, yielding a third option, usually seen when the premise itself is not true. An example of this may be an argument that a prehistoric cat had a long tail but upon gathering sufficient evidence the animal was in fact discovered to be a dog with a medium sized tail.

Arguments from ignorance does not mean that one can never possess good reasons for thinking that something does or does not exist. The idea of the lack of evidence of existence was captured by philosopher Bertrand Russell in his teapot hypothesis of a china teapot revolving about the sun between Earth and Mars. Russell's teapot, sometimes called the celestial teapot or cosmic teapot, is an analogy first presented by the philosopher Bertrand Russell (1872–1970) to illustrate that the philosophic burden of proof lies upon a person making a claim rather than shifting the burden of proof to others to prove the claim wrong. He was addressing his skepticism in the area of religion. Russell wrote that if he claims that a teapot orbits the Sun somewhere in space between the Earth and Mars, it is nonsensical for him to expect others to believe him on the grounds that they cannot prove him wrong. Russell's teapot is still referred to in discussions concerning the existence of God.

In an article titled "Is There a God?" commissioned, but never published, by Illustrated magazine in 1952, Russell wrote: "Many orthodox people speak as though it were the business of skeptics to disprove received dogmas rather than of dogmatists to prove them. This is, of course, a mistake. If I were to suggest that between the Earth and Mars there is a china teapot revolving about the sun in an elliptical orbit, nobody would be able to disprove my assertion provided I were careful to add that the teapot is too small to be revealed even by our most powerful telescopes. But if I were to go on to say that, since my assertion cannot be disproved, it is intolerable presumption on the part of human reason to doubt it, I should rightly be thought to be talking nonsense. If, however, the existence of such a teapot were affirmed in ancient books, taught as the sacred truth every Sunday, and instilled into the minds of children at school, hesitation to believe in its existence would become a mark of eccentricity and entitle the doubter to the attentions of the psychiatrist in an enlightened age or of the Inquisitor in an earlier time."

In 1958, Russell elaborated on the analogy.
"I ought to call myself an agnostic; but, for all practical purposes, I am an atheist. I do not think the existence of the Christian God any more probable than the existence of the Gods of Olympus or Valhalla. To take another illustration: nobody can prove that there is not between the Earth and Mars a china teapot revolving in an elliptical orbit, but nobody thinks this sufficiently likely to be taken into account in practice. I think the Christian God just as unlikely."

Absence of evidence is not *proof* of absence. To make a statement that cannot be proven false does not make it true. Thus we stand here in the balanced philosophical point asking the question posed by so many and reasonably answered by so few. Just because the Bible does not speak about a subject does not mean the subject did not exist. Conversely, simply because the Bible mentions something does not mean it exists.

In 1611, when the KJV was produced, the translators used the word "unicorn" to translate a single Hebrew word, רְאֵם reym, because they didn't know what the original Hebrew word meant. It is the English that critics complain about, not the original Hebrew text. Let's take a look at a few of the verses in the KJV that use the word "unicorn."

Job. 39:9-10 KJV, "Will the unicorn be willing to serve thee, or abide by thy crib? 10Canst thou bind the unicorn with his band in the furrow? or will he harrow the valleys after thee?"

Psalm 22:21 KJV, "Save me from the lion's mouth: for thou hast heard me from the horns of the unicorns."

Isaiah 34:7 KJV, "And the unicorns shall come down with them, and the bullocks with the bulls; and their land shall be soaked with blood, and their dust made fat with fatness."

It is possible the Hebrew word refers to the great aurochs or wild bulls, which are now extinct, however the exact meaning is not known. Nevertheless, the KJV mentions unicorns and they do not exist.

There are a myriad of animals, items, and situations not mentioned in the Bible that exist, thus simply because something is not mentioned does not mean it is absent or nonexistent.

The search for proof opens up the grand argument about what is acceptable evidence. What is proof? How much circumstantial evidence must be piled up to win the argument of the day? When dealing with history, or any situation where the context of evidence is lost, what constitutes reliable testimony? Can one examine myth and legend to uncover truth? Many people believe that the Bible itself is full of embellishment and myth. All input must be weighed according to its probable authenticity. The reader is more than intelligent enough to do this if the sources are identified.

Was there a historical figure named Jesus of Nazareth? We have sufficient evidence confirming the existence of Jesus of Nazareth, but did this man, Jesus, have a wife, and if he did was that spouse Mary of Magdala? Who was this Mary Magdalene? Were there social or religious conditions at the time of Jesus that can give us clues? Are there sources we can draw upon to give us a glimpse into the world of Jesus and Mary?

We have clouded our views by assumptions and traditional beliefs regarding Jesus and Mary. Some of these are based on unfounded assertions and mistakes that have been passed down long enough to be held as truth. Some are misunderstandings regarding society and history. The most stubborn are the incorrect religious views which have made it into our dogma.

It has been long taught that Mary was a prostitute. We have asserted that this man, Jesus, is God and we have asserted that God should not be married in his mortal, earthly form as Jesus. Yet, there are contrary views of both Jesus and Mary, which are just as plausible and easier to prove.

Yet, this is the rub, that history cannot be "proven" as one proves a scientific theory by tests and reproducible experimentation. History is "proven" only by a preponderance of evidence correctly interpreted in the correct context. Premise, evidence, and context must align in a logical, reasonable way based on known social, historical knowledge, which is itself built upon the same reasoned alignment of evidence, usually gathered through ancient texts and archeological digs.

Let us approach the question of the marital status of Jesus and Mary by first clearing away any religious belief, story and myth not backed up by evidence or data, either written or archeological. This does not mean we cannot use the Bible as input. Indeed, it is a valid source when taken in context with other data supplied by archeology and other historical documents. Let us look afresh at Bibles and books, customs and society, as well as physical evidence and ancient writings in an honest attempt to uncover the truth. Let us also be keenly aware that in the end we will have only our best investigative guess as to the historical truth based on the evidence available and interpretation thereof.

New Evidence - Was Jesus Married?

In 2011 Dr. Karen King was given a fragment of papyrus written in Coptic. She received the item from a man she is yet to identify to the public. In September of 2012, King unveiled the fourth century Coptic text containing a reference to the wife of Jesus. The scrap of papyrus rekindled intense speculation and discussion about the life of the founder of Christianity.

Karen L. King is the Hollis professor of divinity at Harvard, the oldest endowed chair in the United States and one of the most prestigious chairs in religious studies. King has been on the forefront of challenging the history of biblical Christianity. She has written that "the traditional history of Christianity is written almost solely from the viewpoint of the side that won, which was successful in silencing other voices, destroying and suppressing any who disagreed with them as 'heretics.'" If one were to look for a person to give an eye to a controversial document King would be a good choice.

King admits, "if authentic, the fragment was written over 300 years after Jesus' death and does not prove that Jesus was married. " However, that is what the content of the document seems to state outright by Jesus himself. Adding to the controversy of the fragment is that its owner, who collects Greek, Coptic and Arabic papyri, is not willing to be identified either by name, nationality or location, nor has information been released as to when, where and how the fragment was discovered.

The piece of document is about the size of a business card and contains 8 partial lines with about 33 words. It dates to the 4th century C.E. or about 300 years after Jesus lived. Although the Coptic text is dated much too late to reflect any eyewitness description of the life of Jesus, it does reflect deep thought and concern about Jesus' marital status in the time it was penned.

The "Gospel of Jesus' Wife", the names that Karen King attached to the item, was written on a torn and frayed square of papyrus. A picture of the fragment is below.

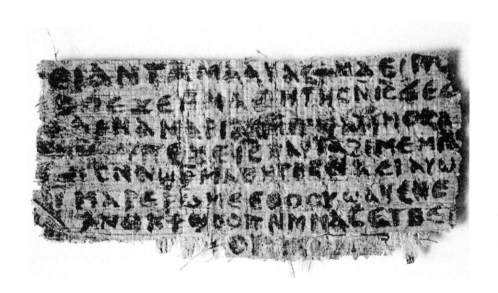

King believes the scrap is the first ancient evidence of Jesus speaking directly of a wife, however it has ignited a firestorm of controversy regarding its authenticity. Two Coptic scholars, AnneMarie Luijendijk of Princeton University and Roger Bagnall of New York University, considered the text authentic and dating back to the fourth century, according to the Biblical Archaeology Society's spokesperson. However, in weeks following the announcement, several scholars voiced their concerns the papyrus was a fake.

Bernhard, author of "Other Early Christian Gospels" (T & T Clark, 2006), brought attention, in a paper published online, to similarities such as grammatical errors and line breaks that have been found only in flawed online translation of the Gospel of Thomas. He points to these errors as evidence that the item is a forgery copied by a person who was not fluent in Coptic.

The Gospel of Jesus' Wife, Bernhard found, seems to be the work of an amateur who pieced together individual words and phrases from Michael Grondin's "Interlinear Coptic-English Translation of the Gospel of Thomas." Authenticity may not be established until further analysis has been conducted.

Dr. King announced her research in the Vatican's front yard at a Coptic Studies conference at the Catholic Church's Institutum Patristicum Augustinianum in Rome. King submitted her paper to the *Harvard Theological Review*, which asked three scholars to review it. Two of the three questioned its authenticity, but they had seen only low-resolution photographs of the fragment and one of the two questioned the grammar, as well as King's translation and interpretation. Due to the controversy over authenticity the article, which was scheduled to be published in January 2013, has been canceled.

King's 2003 book, *The Gospel of Mary of Magdala: Jesus and the First Woman Apostle,* argued, among other things, that Mary was the model of apostleship. King sees the Coptic fragment as fresh evidence of the diversity of voices in early Christianity. Despite her provocative title about the Coptic fragment, King suggests that "This new gospel doesn't prove that Jesus was married, but it tells us that the whole question only came up as part of vociferous debates about sexuality and marriage." If Jesus was married, King does not argue that Jesus was married to Mary Magdalene.

This small fragment does not prove Jesus was married. If it is indeed proven to be authentic and the spectrum analysis of the ink confirms this, this fragment probably says more about Gnosticism than it does biblical Christianity. This text, along with the Gospel of Mary Magdalene, the Gospel of Philip, and the Gospel of Thomas, have been used by King to make the case that there was an alternative version of Christianity that indicated a great deal more diversity in the early centuries of Christianity. However, all of these texts indicate the possibility of Jesus being married. We shall examine these Gnostic gospels as we build our body of evidence.

recto (along the fibres →)

Transcription	Translation
1 ⲡⲁϫⲉⲓ ⲁⲛ ⲧⲁⲙⲁⲁⲩ ⲁⲥϯ ⲛⲁⲉⲓ ⲡⲱⲛ̣ⲏ̣	1] "not [to] me. My mother gave to me li[fe…"
2]ⲉ ⲡⲉϫⲉ ⲙ̄ⲙⲁⲑⲏⲧⲏⲥ ⲛ̄ⲓ̄ⲥ̄ ϫⲉ ⲥ̣[	2] The disciples said to Jesus, ".[
3]. ⲁⲣⲛⲁ ⲙⲁⲣⲓⲁⲙ ⲙ̄ⲡϣⲁ ⲙ̄ⲙⲟⲥ ⲁ̣[ⲛ(?)	3] deny. Mary is worthy of it* [
4]. . . . . ⲛ̄ ⲡⲉϫⲉ ⲓ̄ⲥ̄ ⲛⲁⲩ ⲧⲁϩⲓⲙⲉ ⲙ̄ⲛ̣[	4]……" Jesus said to them, "My wife . .[
5]. . . ⲥⲛⲁϣⲣ̄ⲙⲁⲑⲏⲧⲏⲥ ⲛⲁⲉⲓ ⲁⲩⲱ [	5]… she will be able to be my disciple . . [
6]ϯ ⲙ̄ⲁⲣⲉⲡⲣⲱⲙⲉ ⲉⲑⲟⲟⲩ ϣⲁϥⲉ ⲛⲉ̣[	6] Let wicked people swell up … [
7]. ⲁⲛⲟⲕ ϯϣⲟⲟⲡ ⲛⲙ̄ⲙⲁⲥ ⲉⲧⲃⲉ ⲡ̣[	7] As for me, I dwell with her in order to . [
8 papyrus broken off ↑6] .ⲟⲩϩⲓⲕⲱⲛ . .[	8] an image [
9 (illegible traces of ink)	

* Or alternatively: Mary is n[ot] worthy of it.

The translation of the Gospel of Jesus' Wife is printed in bold font below.

King and other Coptic experts translated the papyrus's eight lines of text, which are cut off at both ends, and read as follows:

1) ... not [to] me, my mother gave to me li[fe] ...

2) The disciples said to Jesus, "...

3) ... deny. Mary is worthy of it ... (or, alternatively, Mary is not worth of it ...) *

4) ..." Jesus said to them, "My wife ...

5) ... she will be able to be my disciple ...

6) Let wicked people swell up ...

7) As for me, I dwell with her in order to ...

8) ... an image ...

* The word to make this statement a negative is in a place in the line, which is missing. In such a case it is impossible to tell if the statement is "Mary is worthy of it" or " Mary is worthy of it not".

Excerpts from the paper submitted by Dr. Karen King

The paper delivered to the Vatican by Karen King:
"Jesus said to them, 'My wife...'"

A New Coptic Gospel Papyrus

by Karen L. King with contributions by AnneMarie Luijendijk
Copyright © Karen L. King, 2012

Published here for the first time is a fragment of a fourth-century CE codex in Coptic containing a dialogue between Jesus and his disciples in which Jesus speaks of "my wife." This is the only extant ancient text which explicitly portrays Jesus as referring to a wife. It does not, however, provide evidence that the historical Jesus was married, given the late date of the fragment and the probable date of original composition only in the second half of the second century. Nevertheless, if the second century date of composition is correct, the fragment does provide direct evidence that claims about Jesus' marital status first arose over a century after the death of Jesus in the context of intra-Christian controversies over sexuality, marriage, and discipleship. Just as Clement of Alexandria (d. ca 215 C.E.) described some Christians who insisted Jesus was not married, this fragment suggests that other Christians of that period were claiming that he was married. For purposes of reference, the fragment is referred to as The Gospel of Jesus's Wife (GosJesWife).

The papyrus currently belongs to a private collector. Assuming it authenticity for the moment, its language (Sahidic Coptic) as well as the conditions for the preservation of organic material indicate that it was found in Egypt. Nothing is known about the circumstances of its discovery, but we have some clues about its modern history. The current owner possesses a typed and signed letter addressed to H. U. Laukamp dated July 15, 1982, from Prof. Dr. Peter Munro (Freie Universität, Ägyptologisches Seminar, Berlin). The letter states that a colleague, Prof. Fecht, has identified one of Mr. Laukamp's papyri as a 2nd-4th c. C.E. fragment of the Gospel of John in Coptic. He advises that this fragment be preserved between glass plates in order to protect it from further damage. This fragment of the Gospel of John is now in the collection of the owner of *GosJesWife*, who acquired it among the same batch of Greek and Coptic papyri.

We wish to offer here our sincerest thanks to the owner, who wishes to remain anonymous, for permission to publish this papyrus fragment...

"Professor Fecht believes that the small fragment, approximately 8 cm in size, is the sole example of a text in which Jesus uses direct speech with reference to having a wife. Fecht is of the opinion that this could be evidence for a possible marriage." ...

(End of Excerpts)

Jesus and Mary

There is nothing totally new in the discovery of a fourth-century papyrus fragment indicating that Jesus was married. The "Gnostic Gospels," which were written by early Christian sects and uncovered in the Egyptian desert in 1945 ("Nag Hammadi Library"), also reported a romantic relationship -- and possibly marriage -- between Jesus and Mary Magdalene. The Gospel of Philip says:

"There were three who always walked with the Lord: Mary, his mother, and her sister, and Magdalene, the one who was called his companion."

The complete Gospel of Philip is included in this book for your further study.

Another passage from this Gospel is even more explicit about Mary Magdalene:

"[Jesus] loved her more than all the disciples, and used to kiss her often on her (mouth). The rest of the disciples said to him, why do you love her more than all of us?"

Note that the word "mouth" is actually not clear in the text but is missing due to damage. It is assumed the word belonging in the sentence is "mouth".

The Gospel of Mary, found in the 19th century near Akhmim in upper Egypt, also describes a special relationship between Jesus and Mary Magdalene:

"Peter said to Mary, Sister we know that the Savior loved you more than the rest of women. Tell us the words of the Savior which you remember which you know, but we do not, nor have we heard them."

The Gospel of Mary Magdalene is also included in this book for your further study.

In the Gospel of Thomas, on of the oldest records of Jesus we have and likely penned before the four gospels of Matthew, Mark, Luke, and John, we read in verse 114:

"Simon Peter said to them: Send Mary away from us, for women are not worthy of this life. Jesus said: See, I will draw her into me so that I make her male, in order that she herself will become a living spirit like you males. For every female who becomes male will enter the Kingdom of the Heavens"

The Gospel of Thomas is included in its entirety in the back of this book.

Now, we add to the mounting evidence the Gospel of Jesus' Wife wherein Jesus himself says:

..." Jesus said to them, "My wife ...
... she will be able to be my disciple ...

Mention of a special relationship between Jesus and Mary is repeated time and time again. Religious documents are rife with such allusions, but there is a problem. Most of the literature mentioning a relationship seems to be written between 200 CE and 400 CE, occurring in the Gnostic writings. Were they drawing on oral traditions and stories passed down that the church wanted to keep hidden or were the stories fabricated to bolster their views of Christianity? Christianity at this time had several faces. Which, if any, was the true one?

The existence of such themes of Jesus and his wife recur in ancient Christian writings and speak to the fact that marriage and children were very important in the lives of Jews, who embraced the Old Testament dictum: "Be fruitful and multiply" (Genesis 9:7). It was expected that a rabbi would be married and have a family. How else would one know what direction and support to give those in his synagogue?

All the great rabbis were married and had children. Jesus and his disciples were dedicated practicing Jews. The Bible tells us that Jesus never broke any edicts or commandments of God. Many would assume that would include the first command given by God, to multiply. The argument for the fact that Jesus was married draws upon this tradition.

We know that Peter was married. The Gospels of Matthew, Mark and Luke tell us that Jesus visited Peter's mother-in-law and healed her: "And when Jesus was come into Peter's house, he saw his wife's mother laid and sick of a fever. And he touched her hand, and the fever left her: and she arose, and ministered unto them" (Matthew 8:14-15; similar citations in the Gospels of Mark and Luke). There is no question about Peter being married and according to Catholic tradition Peter was designated by Jesus as the one who would lead the disciples: "And I say also unto thee, That thou art Peter, and upon this rock I will build my church" (Mathew 16:18). (Some argue it was the truth Peter spoke that was the rock the church was built upon and not the man himself.)

There continues to be debate over Paul's marital status. There is a letter attributed to St. Ignatius the Martyr, which contains the following: "I call to mind your sanctity as I do that of Elias, Jeremiah, John the Baptist, and the chosen disciples Timothy, Titus, Evadius, and Clement; yet I do not blame such other of the blessed as were bound in the bonds of marriage, but hope to be found worthy of God in following their footsteps in his kingdom, after the example of Abraham, Isaac, Jacob, Joseph, Isaiah, and the other prophets — of Peter and Paul, and the apostles who were married."

Some assert that the name of St. Paul has been interpolated in this famous letter: however, Turrian and all who have seen the letters of Ignatius in the library of the Vatican acknowledge that St. Paul's name appears there. And Baronius does not deny that this passage is to be found in some Greek manuscripts: Non negamus in quibusdam græcis codicibus. But he asserts that these words have been added by modern Greeks.

This type of argument needs first to be applied to the New Testament en mass in that more than one scholar asserts that almost half of it is not authentic or written by someone other than the described author. Where one draws the line of authenticity may be influenced by tradition and faith.

We can, to some degree, put away the debate of whether Paul was married or not, if the other apostles were married. In Paul's first Epistle to the Corinthians a dialog occurs, which is quite sufficient to prove that many of the other apostles were married:

1 Corinthians 9

New International Version 1984

The Rights of an Apostle

1 Am I not free? Am I not an apostle? Have I not seen Jesus our Lord? Are you not the result of my work in the Lord? 2 Even though I may not be an apostle to others, surely I am to you! For you are the seal of my apostleship in the Lord. 3 This is my defense to those who sit in judgment on me. 4 Don't we have the right to food and drink? 5 Don't we have the right to take a believing wife along with us, as do the other apostles and the Lord's brothers and Cephasa? 6 Or is it only I and Barnabas who must work for a living?

It is clear from this passage that many, if not all the apostles were married, as well as St. Peter. And St. Clement of Alexandria positively declares that St. Paul had a wife.

Jesus himself should have been married, according to common Jewish tradition, in order to be believed by the other married apostles as capable of knowing their lot and how to lead and guide them.

Customs of the Day

When Christians search the Jewish roots for Jesus, the question of marriage and even children should surface quickly. The first commandment of the 613 *mtizvot* or commandments in the Torah is "be fruitful and multiply" (Genesis 1:28). It would have been illogical to expect Jesus, a devout and law abiding Jewish man, would have consciously chosen to be single and thus go against God's first command. As a first century Judean following the Torah, Jesus would have been married. Our problem in following this simply line of reason comes from our social and religious ideas of what the Christ-God would have done. Yet, there is an abundance of evidence that even the followers of Jesus in his lifetime did not think he was God and their idea of a messiah was a person with a mission from God for a purpose, to unite and bring the people into peace and communion with God. It in no way meant he was a celibate superman.

Jews do not have a problem with the historical reality of Jesus. Some may even say he was a prophet, sent by God, but they reject his divinity and they assume a rabbi would be married. The possibility of Jesus having a wife is not very challenging to a Jew.

As with all general statement, there are exceptions to the rule. The exception to the Jewish rule of marriage came in the form of the Essenes — the desert monastic cult that is mentioned along with the

Sadducees and Pharisees in the time of Jesus. They were celibate and are therefore outside any Jewish norm. The teachings of Jesus have some similarities to those of the Essense, but there are many divergent teachings also. Because of the differences we assume he was influenced by their teachings but was not part of the group.

What Christians hold up as the lifestyle and teaching of Jesus places him outside the orthodox teachings of all major Jewish groups of the time. So, for Christians to hold an honest dialog about Jesus they must give up one or more of the usual points so often espoused.

On one hand, Jesus was human and either lived as a Jewish man, following what was both law and custom, or he was outside the Jewish norm and did not follow all the laws and customs.

On the other hand the probability or necessity of Jesus, the Judean, Galilean rabbi, being married is not palatable or possible because Christ Jesus the God-man could not have married, at least according to how most Christian perceive it. This position may speak more to our Victorian feelings about sex and marriage than to the divinity of Jesus.

A Jewish mindset would insist that Jesus would have been married, but Christians battle continually with an imposed dichotomy of the Jesus of humanity and the Christ of divinity.

Let us begin our examination by stating the obvious, and then going a step farther. The absence of evidence is not the evidence of absence. Just because the scriptures are silent on the marital status of Jesus does not mean he was not married, nor does it mean he was not single. Now, let us look at what evidence we have and let the reader decide what is acceptable evidence and what is not.

The apostle Peter was married since the Gospels of Matthew, Mark and Luke all speak of Christ healing Peter's mother-in-law, who was suffering from a fever.

In Paul's first letter to the Corinthians (9:5), he asks, "Do we not have the right to take along a Christian wife, as do the rest of the apostles ...?"

From that passage, and from the early writings of the church fathers, it seems probable that all of the apostles were married when they were called by Jesus (with the possible exception of John, who seems to have been very young when chosen).

Clement of Alexandria, for example, wrote, "Peter and Philip fathered children, and Philip gave his daughters in marriage." This would be consistent, too, with the custom of that period in history, when it would have been quite unusual for a man to be unmarried.

In the earliest centuries of the church's history, until around 1000 CE, it was commonplace for clergy to be married. Paul's directive in his first letter to Timothy (3:2) that "a bishop should be irreproachable, married only once."

Things began to change and by the fourth century, when the Council of Elvira was held in Spain, it seems clear that celibacy was already commonplace among Christian clergy, though it never became an absolute mandate for the Latin-rite church until the 11th century. The church began to first encourage and then demand celibacy from its clergy. The reason may be more simple than one would wish to believe. It was common practice at the time for a family to place one son into the clergy. If that son was bequeathed a portion of the family's inheritance after death of the father, and the son was not married but to the church, the church would rightfully claim all inheritance left to the son who was a priest. The church became very rich, absorbing portion after portion from each family.

Celibacy was enforced only after 1100 CE and was not part of the original teachings of the church and certainly not within the teachings of Jesus.

That is not to say all who followed Jesus were definitely married. Paul and Barnabas may have been unmarried, or at least that they traveled without wives. There is some disagreement over whether or not Paul had been married at an earlier point in his life but was in fact a widower at the time of his writing.

1. Paul puts himself in the category of being "unmarried" in 1 Corinthians 7:8 *"I say to the unmarried and to widows that it is good for them if they remain even as I."*

Others had wives, and they took them with them, and expected provision to be made for them. They did this in good conscious showing they supported their families and were sent of God.

1 Corinthians 9

Amplified Bible (AMP)

9 Am I not an apostle (a special messenger)? Am I not free (unrestrained and exempt from any obligation)? Have I not seen Jesus our Lord? Are you [yourselves] not [the product and proof of] my workmanship in the Lord?

2 Even if I am not considered an apostle (a special messenger) by others, at least I am one to you; for you are the seal (the certificate, the living evidence) of my apostleship in the Lord [confirming and authenticating it].

3 This is my [real ground of] defense (my vindication of myself) to those who would put me on trial and cross-examine me.

4 Have we not the right to our food and drink [at the expense of the churches]?

5 Have we not the right also to take along with us a Christian sister as wife, as do the other apostles and the Lord's brothers and Cephas (Peter)?

6 Or is it only Barnabas and I who have no right to refrain from doing manual labor for a livelihood [in order to go about the work of the ministry]?

7 [Consider this:] What soldier at any time serves at his own expense? Who plants a vineyard and does not eat any of the fruit of it? Who tends a flock and does not partake of the milk of the flock?

8 Do I say this only on human authority and as a man reasons? Does not the Law endorse the same principle?

Actually, bishops and elders were supposed to have a wife and children to demonstrate they could handle a church as Paul wrote (Roman Catholic approved Rheims New Testament throughout except as otherwise noted):

1.FAITHFUL saying. If a man desire a Bishops office, he desireth a good work.

2. It behoveth therefore a Bishop to be irreprehensible, the husband of one wife,

sober, wise, comely, chaste, a man of hospitality, a teacher,

3. Not given to wine, no fighter, but modest, no quarreler, not covetous,

4. Well ruling his own house, chaving his children subject with all charity.

5. But if a man know not to rule his own house: how shall he have care of the Church of

God? (1 Timothy 3:1-5).

5. For this cause left I thee in Crete, that thou shouldest reform the things that are

wanting, and shouldst ordain priests by cities, as I also appointed thee:

6. If any be without crime, the husband of one wife, having faithful children, not in the

accusations of riot, or not obedient.

7. For a Bishop must be without crime, as the steward of God: not proud, not angry, nor

given to wine, no striker, nor covetous of filthy lucre (Titus 1:5-7).

Note that the term translated as priest in verse 4, presbyter, simply means elder. Also notice that the Bishop is also allowed to be married.

Perhaps I should mention that the Fuller Theological Seminary historian and scholar Nathan Feldmeth believes that since Paul stated that he was a Pharisee, and that Pharisees had to be married, that Paul probably was married once.

Who Did They Say He Was

We may say that Jesus was different and was not a man but God, but this is not the way he was viewed by those around him or anyone at the time he was alive.

In a time when Jewish Christianity was less refined and organized and followers were faced with defining the major elements of the emergent Christian faith it was the Didache that offered the first text book of worship. Importance is given to the way of life, to prophecy, to communal gatherings, to the apocalypse, and to the soon return of Jesus.

"Jesus Christ" is only mentioned once, during the rite of broken bread (9:3-4). The sharing of eucharistic bread is not the reason for the gathering. There is no mention of the body of Christ (1 Corinthians, 10:17). The breaking of bread is a foretaste and anticipation of the return of Christ and the perfection of self and community his return will bring, when all are united, and the "end time" brings restoration of holiness, peace, and complete harmony with God and His followers.

Christ is not mentioned during the rite of cup (9:2), neither does this title appear in the communal thanksgiving prayer, which is offered after the meal.

During the eucharist (9:2-3, 10:2-3) Jesus is called "servant" (Greek "pais") of the Father and "Christ" (anointed) only once and his connection with the "broken bread" is referenced in 9:4.

The early Christian community believed the beginning of the "end time" and the coming apocalypse was heralded with the arrival and death of Jesus. It is the space of time between then and the return of Jesus that we deal with here.

In the Didache, the traditional Jewish custom of drinking wine, breaking bread and saying thanks after the meal was not made referring to Christ nor was the meal or thanksgiving looking to the relationship between bread and wine and the Body and Blood of the "Son of God". The love-meal (agape) was rooted in the eucharist but became isolated only after the ritual meal of Judaism and the eucharist were separated. At the time there were many pagan religions conducting rituals in which there was symbolic eating of the "flesh" of a sacrificial victim or "god". The ceremony was common throughout the Middle East with the mystery cults, Mithraism, Isis and Osiris, Greek mysteries and other religious festivals. The rituals proposed in the Didache are not about this pagan practice but are firmly rooted in the tradition of Jewish prayer and community. Didache 10 is suggestive of the "birkat ha-mazon", a thanksgiving prayer at the end of the Jewish supper.

There is no mention that Christ is god who came in the flesh and died on the cross for our sins. This notion became the basis for the Christian Mass later.

Even Peter declares him to be the Messiah, but not God.

NIV

Matthew 16: 13 When Jesus came to the region of Caesarea Philippi, he asked his disciples, "Who do people say the Son of Man is?"

14 They replied, "Some say John the Baptist; others say Elijah; and still others, Jeremiah or one of the prophets."

15 "But what about you?" he asked. "Who do you say I am?"

16 Simon Peter answered, "You are the Messiah, the Son of the living God."

(It should be noted, as odd as it may seem to modern Christians, that there were those who believed that Jesus was born of a virgin but still rejected his divinity. One idea does not follow the other.)

The disagreement between Eastern and Western Christianity as to the precise moment that consecration of the host happens within the Mass (both positions being without empirical proof) caused a schism between Eastern and Western Christianity. The West believes at the mention of "the Son" there is consecration (and transubstantiation), whereas the East invokes the Holy Spirit to effect the change of the substances of the Eucharist.

There are traces of Q-material in the Didache, which indicates that the Didache is independent of the seed document Matthew and Luke drew upon, which most believe was the Gospel of Mark, or the notes and traditions which gave rise to Mark. Perhaps the Didache helps to explain the background behind the gospel texts. The Didache suggests an independence from the synoptic Gospels and so throws light on the text of these gospels. This may confirm that the sayings of Jesus were collected in a written form. These may be the sayings which were later placed into a document of over one hundred sayings of Jesus called, "The Gospel of Thomas." Like the Didache, the Gospel of Thomas is not a narrative gospel but a wisdom discourse.

The information within the text is presented as a wisdom book based on the sayings of Jesus, which is in the Q document, instead of the narrative gospels, which tell a story. There is a parallel between Didache 9:5 where a logia is mentioned and the Gospel of Thomas.

If we examine what became the Lord's Prayer we find it fairly intact.
"When you pray, say :
'Father, may Your Name be holy.
May Your rule take place.
Always give us our bread.
Forgive us our debts,
for we ourselves forgive everyone that is indebted to us.
And lead us away from a trying situation'."
Q1, logia 42-44.

The word "epiousios" (8:2) is usually translated as "daily". This translation is somewhat arbitrary but became ubiquitous and thus the accepted rendering. The word "epiousion" has "epi" and "ousia as its parts. Epi means, "it is present" or "it happens". "Ousia" means "substance or essence". It refers to the "bread". If "epiousion" is understood as a "spiritual" process happening with the bread, then this word can be read as, "Give us now our spiritual bread."

The early Christians believed that Christ would come back within their lifetime. Their liturgies served to remind them of the imminent return. The love feast or Eucharist was not part of His death as it is today. There was no interpretation of "bread" as the "Body of Christ", nor is there a trace of the "this is My body" - "this is My blood". The meal - the Eucharist - was a gathering and a meal as a rehearsal and reminder of what communal unity and love was to come. To experience the presence of Christ by anticipating his return is evidenced in the Didache. This is the only text we have containing liturgical information about the Q-communities, of which the Essenes belonged.

The Didache shows little to no "Pauline" Christianity. Paul would have been present but his influence had not yet been fully established. It was James, the brother of Jesus, who was the "heir apparent" after the death of Jesus. James headed the Jewish Christian movement. Although Peter may have had a high status it was James who became the head of the Christian church or ministry in Jerusalem, which was considered the holiest position at the time. James wished to continue closer to the line of Judaism but Paul wished to reach out to the Pagan Gentile population. Later, the Catholic Church would view Peter as the apostle of succession and attempt to trace the papal lineage back to him, however Paul, it seems, had the greatest influence on Christianity and much of our faith today is Christianity as interpreted by Paul.

In the Book of Acts we are told Paul and Barnabas came back to Jerusalem to speak to the Apostles. The apostles, led by James, gave them a list of things to do. It was an odd list.

Acts 15:*29 You are to abstain from food sacrificed to idols, from blood, from the meat of strangled animals and from sexual immorality. You will do well to avoid these things.*
 Farewell.

The major problem between Jews and the Gentile converts had to do with the Gentile's continuation to worship their idols and act according to that worship instead of the Christian way. All recommendations have a connection with pagan idol worship, of which sex acts and various forms of animal sacrifice and feast were part. The Jews brought the Old Testament to their attention.

Ex 20:2-6

2 I am the LORD your God, who brought you out of Egypt, out of the land of slavery.

3 You shall have no other gods before me.

4 You shall not make for yourself an idol in the form of anything in heaven above or on the earth beneath or in the waters below.

5You shall not bow down to them or worship them; for I, the LORD your God, am a jealous God, punishing the children for the sin of the fathers to the third and fourth generation of those who hate me,

6but showing love to a thousand [generations] of those who love me and keep my commandments.

Other "suggestions" are based on the 7th commandment and the Gentile's immorality. This is because such immorality was connected to idol worship.

Ex 20:14

"You shall not commit adultery.

The list of restrictions aimed at the Gentiles addressed only the major issues so the other commandments were not discussed. The Gentiles were not given license to break the other commandments. It was simply that those other offenses were not an issue.

All recommendations were based on common practices among the Gentiles who were recently converted. Gentiles couldn't eat the food and drinks of close friends and relatives who sacrificed to idols.

Gentiles did not have to be circumcised to prove that they were Christians, but they had to avoid continuing certain practices. In other words, Gentile Christians should not have to become officially like their Jewish brethren through circumcision, but they should avoid identifying themselves as pagans through practices.

In the early days of Christianity the movement was considered an offshoot sect of Judaism. Soon the main trunk of the sect began to split into three major branches, although even these main branches soon began to splinter. We will first look at the main divisions and discuss the minor differences within the subdivisions later.

The Didache captures a snapshot of Christianity before it was infiltrated with the pagan religions, which surrounded the areas of Christian concentration, Jerusalem and Rome.

One of the main influences was the religion of Mithras.
Virtually all of the elements of Orthodox Christian rituals, from miter, wafer, water baptism, alter, and doxology, were adopted from the Mithras and earlier pagan mystery religions. The religion of Mithras preceded Christianity by roughly six hundred years. However, it was very active in Rome from the 1st to 4th centuries C.E.

(1) According to the Mithras myth, Mithras was born on December 25th as an offspring of the Sun. Next to the gods Ormuzd and

Ahrimanes, Mithras held the highest rank among the gods of ancient Persia. He was represented as a beautiful youth and a Mediator. Reverend J. W. Lake states: "Mithras is spiritual light contending with spiritual darkness, and through his labors the kingdom of darkness shall be lit with heaven's own light; the Eternal will receive all things back into his favor, the world will be redeemed to God. The impure are to be purified, and the evil made good, through the mediation of Mithras, the reconciler of Ormuzd and Ahriman. Mithras is the Good, his name is Love. In relation to the Eternal he is the source of grace, in relation to man he is the life-giver and mediator" (Plato, Philo, and Paul, p. 15).

(2) Mithras was considered a great teacher and master. He had twelve companions and traveled with performing miracles.

(3) Mithras was called "the good shepherd, "the way, the truth and the light, redeemer, savior, Messiah." He was identified with both the lion and the lamb.

(4) The International Encyclopedia states: "Mithras seems to have owed his prominence to the belief that he was the source of life, and could also redeem the souls of the dead into the better world ... The ceremonies included a sort of baptism to remove sins, anointing, and a sacred meal of bread and water, while a consecrated wine, believed to possess wonderful power, played a prominent part."

(5) Chambers Encyclopedia says: "The most important of his many festivals was his birthday, celebrated on the 25th of December. Baptism and the partaking of a mystical liquid, consisting of flour and water, to be drunk with the utterance of sacred formulas, were among the inauguration acts."

(6) Prof. Franz Cumont, of the University of Ghent, writes as follows concerning the religion of Mithras and the religion of Christ: "Followers of Mithras also held Sunday sacred, and celebrated the birth of the Sun on the 25th of December...." (The Mysteries of Mithras, pp. 190, 191).

(7) Reverend Charles Biggs stated: "The disciples of Mithra formed an organized church, with a developed hierarchy. They possessed the ideas of Mediation, Atonement, and a Savior, who is human and yet divine, and not only the idea, but a doctrine of the future life. They had a Eucharist, and a Baptism, and other curious analogies might be pointed out between their system and the church of Christ (The Christian Platonists, p. 240).

(8) In Roman catacombs a relic of Mithraic worship was preserved. It was a picture of the infant Mithras seated in the lap of his virgin mother, while on their knees before him were Persian Magi adoring him and offering gifts.

(9) He was buried in a tomb and after three days he rose again. His resurrection was celebrated every year.

(10) The Christian Father Manes, founder of the heretical sect known as Manicheans, believed that Christ and Mithras were one. His teaching, according to Mosheim, was as follows: "Christ is that glorious intelligence which the Persians called Mithras ... His residence is in the sun" (Ecclesiastical History, 3rd century, Part 2, ch. 5).

We can see from the above list that there may have been a "cross-pollination" of stories and myths between religions. We must take care not to throw out truth simply because it is mimicked in paganism. Just because a pattern occurs in another religion, it does not make the pattern in Christianity incorrect. We must simply strip off the contamination to find the original and true belief system.

Above all, to discover the unsullied core of Christianity we dare not go past the Counsel of Nicaea. The Emperor Constantine was thought to be a follower of Mithras who adopted Christianity as a matter of expediency for the purpose of uniting and controlling his subjects, the majority of whom were Christian. While forging this unity he was active in the formation of modern Christian doctrines, such as the trinity. The creed produced under his watchful eye confirms several beliefs held by the followers of Mithras, and likely held by the emperor himself.

Those who stayed with the roots of the Jesus movement were mostly Jewish converts. Many were still worshipping in synagogues. The Jewish Christians viewed it as their duty to love God and Neighbor, serve the community, and pray for their enemies. They accepted Jesus as the anointed servant of God and the one sent to mediate between God and man (in the way of a priest) and teach us how to live in order to please God, but they did not accept that Jesus was God, nor did the idea of his death paying for our sin occur to them. To this group it was their faith in God and following the teachings of Jesus regarding the way one treated others and loved God that was the path to salvation. Jesus was regarded as a man, pure and righteous enough that he could communicate with God and talk to the people. Thus, he was the mediator. In the end the people of his time knew it was God who would bring Jesus back to them, just as Jews still look for the return of Elijah today and leave a place set for him at their tables.

Another group who combined various Greek philosophies with the new faith were Gnostics. They believed this world was evil and the body entrapped the spirit. Salvation was realizing the truth that the material world was the enemy of the spiritual world. Jesus was sent to teach the people who the real God was and that the spirit world was the most important realm.

Then there was "Pauline Christianity." This is what the church practices today. James and most of the other apostles did not subscribe to many of Paul's interpretations of Christianity. Paul had never met Jesus before Jesus' death and resurrection and was a late-comer to the faith, although he claimed to have spent time in the desert where the ascended Jesus appeared and instructed him. Did Paul really know the intent of Jesus better than believers who grew up with him, such as his brother, who was now over the main Christian church? Paul taught that faith and faith alone brought salvation to the convert. The faith demanded was one focused on the fact that Jesus was sent by God to die in our place and thus take our place in the hands of a God who, without seeing such a faith would assign a place in hell to those who violated the least of the Old Testament laws. Paul rejected the Old Testament laws and rituals for those who were saved. Did James and the others misunderstand exactly who and what Jesus was? Was Jesus, the prophet, without honor in his own land? Or, did Paul hijack Christianity by imposing his own interpretations of faith, grace, works, and redemption?

The spilling of blood and the sacrifice of Jesus as the payment of sin is not mentioned in the Didache. Jesus is the Messiah, the Christ, the anointed one, the servant of God, but not God in the flesh. The Holy Spirit is mentioned as the baptism is done in the name of the Father, Son, and Holy Spirit. This forces us to discern the difference between the Spirit of God and God, who is a spirit.

The Didache gives simple instruction to the initiates for their entrance into the community and their salvation:

47

Show love toward your neighbor and enemies.

Abstain from lusts.

Give to the needy and show compassion to others.

Do not murder, Do not commit adultery, Do not have illicit sex, Do not steal, Do not commit abortion or infanticide.

Do not be prone to anger.

Do not engage in sorcery, witchcraft, enchantings, astrology. (This refers to potions, drugs, spells, dealing with spirits of the dead or evil spirits, or attempting to foretell the future.)

Share all things with your brothers and sisters.

Do not eat food that was sacrificed to idols.

Baptize in living (running, fresh) water in the name of the Father, Son and Holy Spirit.

Fast on the 4th day of the week.

Recite the Our Father prayer three times a day.

Beware of and reject false prophets.

Elect honorable Christians to be bishops and deacons to oversee the members.

Be ready at all times for the return of Jesus, who is the servant of God and the mediator who came to teach us how to live, worship, and commune.

The idea of Jesus coming again follows along the same idea as the return of Elijah, for whom a place is still set in Jewish homes today. It does not make Jesus any more divine than Elijah.

The Didache gives instructions on certain ceremonies. Within the ceremonies of the Eucharist and thanksgiving the place of Jesus in the early church is shown. The cup is first consecrated. Nowhere is the divinity of Jesus Christ mentioned during the Offertory or the Eucharistic prayer. Jesus is only spoken of as "Christ" over the bread, not over the cup. Communion happens before thanksgiving. Thanksgiving does not ask for the consecration of the fully prepared elements since they are no longer present, having been already consumed. Thanksgiving is fully focused on God the Father. Jesus is not mentioned as Christ, nor as Son, but only as a servant of the Father God. Jesus returns to complete the work of gathering and unifying believers in holy peace and communion with God and one another.

In the Dead Sea Scrolls found at Qumrân, we find the following interesting text:

"And when they shall gather for the common table, to eat and to drink new wine, when the common table shall be set for eating and new wine poured for drinking, let no man extend his hand over the first-fruits of bread and wine before the Priest; for it is he who shall bless the first-fruits of bread and wine, and shall be the first to extend his hand over the bread. Thereafter, the Messiah of Israel shall extend his hand over the bread, and all the congregation of the Community shall utter a blessing, each man in the order of his dignity."

The Messianic Rule (1QSa) - translated by Vermes, 1990.

The Didache proves the early Christians believed faith and salvation can exist without the sacrifice of Jesus Christ for our sins. If he was not God he could not be totally perfect. If he was not divinely perfect he would have been an imperfect sacrifice. He was a man, though righteous. During the Eucharist, no mention is made of the sacrifice of Jesus Christ. Only the presence of Christ is needed to raise us spiritually. The idea of Jesus the Christ as the Son of God is not necessary. Jesus is a mediator who serves the Father. It is to God that all of us return and not to Christ. The title of the "Son of God" is used in the Didache when referring to deceivers and in the "Q" when Satan addresses Jesus. The title "Lord" does not justify the trinitarian identification or belief of Jesus Christ as God. This is far too early to entertain the ideas which evolved into the Nicean trinitarian doctrine. The title of "Lord" is used as one of respect. It is the equivalent of "Sir" and was used in the KJV because it was customary at the time.

(The "Q" or source document was used as a common reference in the writing of Matthew, Mark, and Luke. A common source is the only way to explain why there are so many similarities occurring in the same order within the three gospels. It must predate all three gospels. There is more information on "Q" to follow.)

Thanksgiving is directed toward God, the Father, only. It is His Name which the Didache places in the middle. The cup and the "broken bread" refer to Jesus Christ, who is broken in the fashion of torture and murder but who unites his followers with love. His followers sense his return is imminent. He is always the mediator, never the principal subject. This idea is proven over and over again as we read the opening greetings of the Epistles (letters from one believer to another or a group). It is a greeting in the name of God the Father and the Lord Jesus.

Colossians 1

1Paul, an apostle of Jesus Christ by the will of God, and Timotheus our brother,

2To the saints and faithful brethren in Christ which are at Colosse: Grace be unto you, and peace, from God our Father and the Lord Jesus Christ.

1 Corinthians 1

1Paul called to be an apostle of Jesus Christ through the will of God, and Sosthenes our brother,

2Unto the church of God which is at Corinth, to them that are sanctified in Christ Jesus, called to be saints, with all that in every place call upon the name of Jesus Christ our Lord, both their's and our's:

3Grace be unto you, and peace, from God our Father, and from the Lord Jesus Christ.

2 Corinthians 1

1Paul, an apostle of Jesus Christ by the will of God, and Timothy our brother, unto the church of God which is at Corinth, with all the saints which are in all Achaia:

2Grace be to you and peace from God our Father, and from the Lord Jesus Christ.

1 Timothy 1

1Paul, an apostle of Jesus Christ by the commandment of God our Saviour, and Lord Jesus Christ, which is our hope;

2Unto Timothy, my own son in the faith: Grace, mercy, and peace, from God our Father and Jesus Christ our Lord.

2 Timothy 1

1Paul, an apostle of Jesus Christ by the will of God, according to the promise of life which is in Christ Jesus,

2To Timothy, my dearly beloved son: Grace, mercy, and peace, from God the Father and Christ Jesus our Lord.

James 1

1James, a servant of God and of the Lord Jesus Christ, to the twelve tribes which are scattered abroad, greeting.

Jude 1

1Jude, the servant of Jesus Christ, and brother of James, to them that are sanctified by God the Father, and preserved in Jesus Christ, and called:

2Mercy unto you, and peace, and love, be multiplied.

There does not seem to be any trinity here. He was not equal to God. With the exception of the Gospel of John (Jn. 20:28) apostles called Jesus "Lord", not "God". There is evidence that the Gospel of John was written latter (c.a.100C.E.) than the others and was influenced and changed. One may argue that the Gospel is different than the others due to hindsight and a more full revelation, or one may say the difference indicates corruption. Several books have been written arguing that John's Gospel has been changed to communicate trinity and divinity, which were not there in the original intent or wording. The Didache was written many years prior and did not yet attach divinity to Jesus.

The title of "Lord" is an antiquated term used by the translators in 1611 to render a word "kurios" from "kuros" meaning "The owner or controller of a person, a state sovereign, a title of honor such as "Sir". It has continued to indicate a higher spiritual status ever since.

The members of the community who used the Didache were Jewish Christians since they believed Jesus was the servant or anointed one sent from God. For them Jesus Christ saved them when he was anointed and sent as a "servant" of the Father, but not as God Himself. He was a mediator sent from God to teach and lead, not as the propitiation, as we now believe. His teachings, when practiced, simply brought us back into alignment with God's will and approval.

They saw no Trinity and no sacrificial Lamb of God. These first Christians saw Jesus as a servant doing the will of his master and carrying out the orders to teach, unite, mediate, and demonstrate the ideals of a godly life. Here, in the Didache, we see the beginnings and foundation of what men have built into the Christianity of today. It is the structure beneath the gilding.

Why was the teaching of the blood sacrifice of Jesus left out? Why is there no mention of his payment for the remission of our sins? Does the Didache present a salvation founded solely on works? Faith in God is accounted to the believer as righteousness through God's grace. By faith are we saved through grace. Doing the will of God as taught and exemplified by Jesus not only proves and demonstrates our faith, it completes it, fulfils it, and through discipline and the establishment of holy habits the person is changed and strengthened toward unwavering faith.

The relationship between faith and work is explained in detail throughout the Book of James.

James 2:20-24
Common English Bible (CEB)
20 Are you so slow? Do you need to be shown that faith without actions has no value at all? 21 What about Abraham, our father? Wasn't he shown to be righteous through his actions when he offered his son Isaac on the altar? 22 See, his faith was at work along with

his actions. In fact, his faith was made complete by his faithful actions. 23 So the scripture was fulfilled that says, Abraham believed God, and God regarded him as righteous.[a] What is more, Abraham was called God's friend. 24 So you see that a person is shown to be righteous through faithful actions and not through faith alone.

James asked the only relevant question left.

James 2:14

New King James Version (NKJV)

Faith Without Works Is Dead

14 What does it profit, my brethren, if someone says he has faith but does not have works? Can faith save him?

And in another version it reads:

James 2:14

GOD'S WORD Translation (GW)

We Show Our Faith by What We Do

14My brothers and sisters, what good does it do if someone claims to have faith but doesn't do any good things? Can this kind of faith save him?

Does this mean that salvation is not by faith alone? One may argue that if faith without works is dead and meaningless, then it would take both. Thus, according to James there is no Sola Fida (Faith Alone). Now, Sola Scriptura cannot be, for the early Christians are saved, not having the New Testament and Gentiles having neither Old or New Testaments are saved simply by accepting and following Jesus; and Sola Fida falls to the need for works to fulfill it, leaving only Sola Gratia (by Grace alone), for only through God's grace can our faith and acts be accounted to us as righteousness. No amount of work is worth heaven, but by grace our faith blooms into works and God's grace does the rest. As Isaiah 58 says, "All our righteousness are as filthy rags." This is the way the first Christians saw salvation.

Since the beginning of the Christian faith men have fought with themselves and one another to understand the position of faith and works within salvation. Martin Luther was so upset at the stance James took that he rejected the Epistle, calling it a "straw epistle", which he wanted to burn. The only two beliefs constituting the core of all mainstream forms of the faith were the resurrection and the return of Jesus.

In these ideas the Didache and the Book of James walk hand in hand to such a degree that it suggests that James himself, or one of his disciples, could have written Didache 1 – 6. So close is the parallel with the Didache that The Book of James is included in Appendix "A" for the reader to compare after reading the first 6 chapters of the Didache for a fuller understanding of the Book of James.

Many scholars consider the epistle of James to be written in the late 1st or early 2nd centuries, after the death of James the Just. It is thought James may have written a prior version of the letter, which was later polished and completed by one of his disciples. James, being both the leader of the faith and one of the main contributors to the Didache, as the name "The Teaching of the Twelve" indicates, would have helped set the tone of the document. This theory is bolstered by the fact that the Book of James and the Didache are so similar is content. The other apostles, Peter, John, Andrew, James, Matthew, Simon, Thomas, Jude, Philip, James the Less, Bartholomew, and Mathias would have contributed and all would have agreed with the teachings. Paul was not a contributor but came later, taking the title, "Apostle to the Gentiles," a title of specificity, which through circumstance and "mission creep" possibly took on a broader scope in the early church than first intended.

There are parallels between James, 1 Peter, 1 Clement and The Shepherd of Hermas reflecting the political situations Christians were dealing with in the 1st or early 2nd century.

Christianity at the time was primitive and in flux. There were already several sects of Christianity either established or evolving, each having a different idea of who Jesus was. We have discussed three major divisions. Now let us look at others. In the very early days of Christianity, there appear to have been:

Ebionites , meaning "the Poor Ones". They were an early Jewish Christian sect that lived around Judea from the 1st to the 4th century.

This sect of Judæo-Christians believed Jesus was the messiah but they denied his divinity and supernatural origin. They observed all the Jewish rites, such as circumcision and the seventh-day Sabbath and they used the gospel according to Matthew written in Hebrew or Aramaic, but they flatly rejected the writings of Paul as those of an apostate. Some Ebionites accepted the doctrine of the virgin birth of Jesus. Most others did not.

Nazarene means "a Branch". They were an early Jewish Christian sect similar to the Ebionite. They accepted the virgin birth and divinity of Jesus. The term Nazarene was likely the one first used for these followers of Jesus, as evidenced by Acts 24:5 where Paul is called "the ringleader of the sect of the Nazarenes." Thus, these followers were likely folded into the Pauline sect later as Paul continues to develop his Christology. It was at this time that Paul's theology diverged enough from the first Jewish Christians that they discontinued use of the Didache.

The term "Christian," first used in Greek speaking areas for the movement is a translation of the term Nazarene, and basically means a "Messianist."

The Essenes, meaning "Doers of Torah", were the sect which wrote or collected the Dead Sea Scrolls. They were considered part of the collective term called "Way," and existed over 150 years before the birth of Jesus. They baptized as a sign of repentance as entrance requirement into their fellowship.

The Essenes were an apocalyptic group, expecting three redemptive Figures—the Prophet like Moses and his two Messiahs. The sect saw themselves as the remnant of God's people preparing the Way for the return of God's Glory. They formed a tight community and referred to themselves as brother and sister.

They had their own developed interpretation of Torah, some aspects of which Jesus preached. The ideas of no divorce, not using oaths, and the apocalypse are but a few. They followed one they called the True Teacher (Teacher of Righteousness) whom most scholars believe lived in the 1st century B.C.E. but was assassinated by the authorities of the time.

Nazoreans were a first century offshoot of the Essene, according to Epiphanius. There were two branches of Essenes - the Nazoreans and the Ossaeans. Each of these two Essene branches had a monastic part. The monastic part of the northern Nazorean was known as "Children of Amen." The Nazorean B'nai-Amen were also a Monastic Order. It is thought that both Jesus and John the Baptizer were associated with the Essenes and drew some of their doctrine and teachings from them.

Cerinthians followed the Jewish law, denied that the Supreme God had made the physical world, and denied the divinity of Jesus. The doctrine of Cerinthus is stated by Irenaeus in the following passage

Ulcer. i. 26):

" A certain Cerinthus in Asia taught that the world was not made by the Supreme God, but by a certain power entirely separate and distinct from that authority which is above the universe, and ignorant of that God who is over all things. He submitted that Jesus was not born of a virgin (for this seemed to him impossible), but was the son of Joseph and Mary, born as all other men, yet excelling all mankind in righteousness, prudence, and wisdom. And that after His baptism there had descended on Him, from that authority which is above all things, Christ in the form of a dove; and that then He had announced the unknown Father and had worked miracles; but that at the end Christ had flown back again from Jesus, and that Jesus suffered and rose again, but that Christ remained impassible, since He was a spiritual being " (as quoted by A. S. Peake).

Hippolytus adds that Cerinthus taught that the world was made by an angel, and that the Law was given to the Jews by another angel, who was the God of the Jews. These angels were far below the Supreme Being. The teaching of Cerinthus is a mixture of Judaism and Gnosticism.

Carpocratians were an early Gnostic sect founded in the first half of the second century. Carpocrates venerated Jesus, but he also believed that the philosophers Plato, Pythagoras, Aristotle and others were gods. He believed that Jesus was just another man, like any of us, upon whom an extraordinary recollection descended. Carpocrates seems to have placed no faith in anything like the Immaculate Conception, or the virgin birth, but plainly states that Jesus was the son of Joseph. Essentially, Carpocretes believed there was no way to know anything more than what seems obvious.

The first gospels had only recently been written, or were still in the process of revision, but there was a sense that the writings were sacred, however they had not yet been granted canon. The Gnostics were writing their own scriptures. Why not? If there was a gospel written by Mark or Matthew why should there not be a gospel written by Thomas or Baranbas with a Gnostic slant? The Gnostics, being closer to the event of the formation of scripture were less trusting that what the four gospels contained was the untainted word of Christ. The possibility that Jesus was human, like anyone, did not disturb Carpocrates because he saw that the wisdom of Jesus had elevated him to godliness, which was therefore a possibility for anyone who emulated him, after all, Jesus did say we could do all that he did and more.

Carpocrates did not believe that salvation could be obtained only by following Jesus, but that one had to become Jesus (that is to be elevated to a higher spiritual level and become him in spirit) in order to find salvation.

Most Gnostics believed Jesus was the son of Joseph, and was just like other men, but his soul was steadfast and pure, he perfectly remembered those things which he had witnessed within the sphere of the Unbegotten God.

They respected Peter, Paul, and the rest of the apostles, whom they consider to be on an equal spiritual level to Jesus. The Gnostics believed the souls of Peter and Paul descended from the same sphere as that of Jesus.

Some would say that *Pauline Christianity*, with its distinctive theology, was a separate sect. Its followers were probably absorbed into the proto-Catholic-Orthodox sect early in the second century.

The *proto-Catholic-Orthodox* sect is believed to have coexisted with the above sects from the earliest times.
Paul represents only one sect of early Christianity, each vying for converts and attempting to articulate their theology to the exclusion of the others. The Pauline sect was certainly not the "original" one. The original sect and the trunk from which all other sects formed was a messianic Judaism, guided by James. The earliest Christian sect was the Jewish Christianity practiced by Peter, James, and Jesus' earliest followers.

Scholars agree Jesus, his family, his Twelve Apostles, the Elders, and his earliest followers observed the Torah and kept the laws and ceremonies, whereas the main feature of Paul's message was a rejection of the Torah and the Jewish law in order to gain salvation.

Acts chapter 15 suggests two things. It suggests that those who were Jews and converted to the Christian sect continued to practice according to their Jewish roots. It also suggests that even though the apostles gave leniency to the Gentiles, there were those within their group who did not wish to extend the same permission and continued to push the point that Gentiles should become Jews in order to be on equal footing with the apostles, following the Jewish footsteps of Jesus.

Paul's sect came to dominate Christianity partly through the circumstance of politics and partly because entry into the faith was easy, since it was through faith and not following the law. History is written by the winner, so we know little about other sects in earliest Christianity.

Jewish Christians considered Jesus the saving Messiah, but insisted on continued observance of the Jewish laws about ceremony, diet, and circumcision. To some Gentiles the required consent to mutilate their penis was simply too much.

As stated before, James seemed to be the heir apparent to the original Jewish sect of Christianity. James led the Jerusalem church until the Jewish revolt of 66 CE. His commitment to the Torah is recorded by Josephus and by Acts 21:17-21.

The letter of James "to the twelve tribes of the Jewish diaspora" explains how faith produces the works and fruits. These works, which the Torah also demands has a saving function (Jas. 1:21). James mentions Jesus only twice, in incidental ways (1:1 and 2:1). However, James does define what he considers to be the sign of real faith.

Religion that is pure and genuine in the sight of God the Father will show itself by such things as visiting orphans and widows in their distress and keeping oneself uncontaminated by the world. (James 1:27 Phiilip's translation)

Because Paul rejected the authority of the Torah, he wrote against Jewish Christians in 3 of his 7 undisputed letters. This is the main subject of Galatians, and he also warns against "dogs" who insist on circumcision in Phil. 3:2-3, and against those who take pride in their pedigree of being both "Hebrews" and "Israelites" in 2 Cor. 11:5 and 22-23. Paul rejected works as having no part in salvation, but instead insisted that only faith in Jesus could save a person's soul. This was an easier faith to enter and, until one was persecuted, it was an easier religion to live under, having fewer points by which one may be judged.

The Jewish Christians, led by James, had been looking for a Messiah who was a warrior-king. Although the Old Testament told of the torture and death of the messiah the church at this time was divided as to exactly who and what Jesus was. James dismissed the weighty matter of the death of Jesus as a sacrifice for the sins of the world. James, being a devout Jew was looking at Jesus from the Jewish viewpoint of what the Messiah was supposed to be.

According to Jewish scripture and belief, the true Messiah must meet the following requirements.

He must be an observant Jewish man descended from the house of King David.

He must be "The son of man" which is human as opposed to the Son of God.

He must bring peace to the world.

He must gather all Jews back into Israel. (This is usually thought to be through a war.)

He must rebuild the ancient Temple in Jerusalem.

He must convert the world and they will worship the God of Israel. This means observing the Torah and the Law.

The concept of the messiah seems to have developed in later Judaism. The Torah contains very few specific reference to him, though some Jewish scholars have pointed out that it does speak of the "End of Days," which is the time of the messiah.

The Tanakh gives several specifications as to who the messiah will be. He will be a descendent of King David (2 Samuel 7:12-13; Jeremiah 23:5), observant of Jewish law (Isaiah 11:2-5), a righteous judge (Jeremiah 33:15), and a great military leader.

Jews do not believe that the messiah will be divine. A fundamental difference between Judaism and Christianity is the Jewish conviction that God is so essentially different and more holy than humanity that he could not become a human. The messiah is a servant, a man sent by God, a person of pure spirit who can hear from God and speak to mankind. If Jesus was or is God how could he say to us we could do greater works than he did? The fact that the modern church views Jesus as God has stifled believers from performing greater miracles. After all, who could do greater works than God? But if Jesus was a servant, we could be servants of God also and do the same works if not greater. Was this not his message, that we should be like him? He could not ask this of us if he were God.

Moreover, Jews find no foundation in the scriptures for belief in the divinity of the messiah. Passages viewed by Christians as indicating a divine messiah, such as the suffering servant of Isaiah 53, are viewed by Jews as speaking of the people of Israel en masse.

Isaiah 53
New International Version (NIV)

1 Who has believed our message and to whom has the arm of the LORD been revealed? 2 He grew up before him like a tender shoot, and like a root out of dry ground. He had no beauty or majesty to attract us to him, nothing in his appearance that we should desire him. 3 He was despised and rejected by mankind, a man of suffering, and familiar with pain. Like one from whom people hide their faces he was despised, and we held him in low esteem.

4 Surely he took up our pain and bore our suffering, yet we considered him punished by God, stricken by him, and afflicted. 5 But he was pierced for our transgressions, he was crushed for our iniquities; the punishment that brought us peace was on him, and by his wounds we are healed. 6 We all, like sheep, have gone astray, each of us has turned to our own way; and the LORD has laid on him the iniquity of us all.

7 He was oppressed and afflicted, yet he did not open his mouth; he was led like a lamb to the slaughter,   and as a sheep before its shearers is silent, so he did not open his mouth. 8 By oppression and judgment he was taken away. Yet who of his generation protested? For he was cut off from the land of the living; for the transgression of my people he was punished. 9 He was assigned a grave with the wicked, and with the rich in his death, though he had done no violence, nor was any deceit in his mouth.

10 Yet it was the LORD's will to crush him and cause him to suffer, and though the LORD makes his life an offering for sin, he will see his offspring and prolong his days, and the will of the LORD will prosper in his hand. 11 After he has suffered, he will see the light of life and be satisfied; by his knowledge my righteous servant will justify many,   and he will bear their iniquities. 12 Therefore I will give him a portion among the great, and he will divide the spoils with the strong, because he poured out his life unto death, and was numbered with the transgressors. For he bore the sin of many and made intercession for the transgressors.

In Origen's writings, called "Contra Celsus," written in the year 248, he writes of Isaiah 53:
"Now I remember that, on one occasion, at a disputation held with certain Jews, who were reckoned wise men, I quoted these prophecies; to which my Jewish opponent replied, that these predictions bore reference to the whole people, regarded as one individual, and as being in a state of dispersion and suffering, in order that many proselytes might be gained, on account of the dispersion of the Jews among numerous heathen nations."

Owing to the Jewish view of the messiah in the first century it is no wonder that the Didache does not mention the sacrifice of the messiah for the remission of sin.

It is possible the Didache reveals to us the earliest, most pure and simple form of a belief in Jesus as the Christ. There was no mention of the virgin birth, or divinity of Jesus. There is no thought of Jesus being sacrificed for the payment of our sins. There was no rapture, or trinity. There is only a rock-solid belief in Jesus as the messiah sent as a servant of God to be the mediator between God and man. He was the one who was to hear from God and communicate to mankind a way in which we too could commune directly with God. He came to show us how to live.

The Didache is a manual written from the standpoint of the earliest Jewish messianic sect, called "Christians", for the instruction of converts on how to be Christians and how to conduct themselves in daily life. It is a magnificent view of the beliefs and rituals of the earliest form of Christianity as propagated by those who knew Jesus best; his brother and the original apostles.

The Didache, when placed with the "Q" document, will give the reader a vision of what Christianity was like and what Christians believed during the first twenty to thirty years after the death of Jesus.

The questions before us are these:

Did the original twelve apostles have the full truth, were they incorrect, or has the Christian faith been corrupted?

Did the Christian faith evolve into a fuller understanding of God with added beliefs and rituals, or was it subverted and changed into the religion and denominations we have today?

Is the Didache simply history, or is it a way back to the true practice of the faith?

Before we further examine society and customs of the time we must attempt to discern the place Mary and Jesus would have occupied in that society. This will tell us what customs and social constructs they were likely to follow.

One of the best ways to gather information regarding a person is to ask his or her friends. The other way is to ask his or her enemies. Their testimony can point out any sharp divergence or perceived differences between the enemy and the person they are attacking. Friends of Jesus and Mary know them beyond what the gossip has proclaimed. We know that Jesus was a religious leader in his day. We know he had a group of followers, which the local government watched closely for fear they would start an uprising. One of his followers was Mary Magdalene. To get to know the real Jesus and Mary it seems good to look at the earliest writings of their friends and followers.

According to them Jesus is a man. He is a leader. His heart and intentions are thought to be pure and so it is thought that God has chosen him to lead people back to God so they too can hear and obey God. This places him on the same basic level as several other messianic or anointed figures throughout Jewish history. Yet, his followers were less in number than many who came before him. The Didache and a study therein are included in this book.

His enemies tell their stories also. There are letters written by Pilot that mention Jesus and what was going on in the time from a political standpoint. In these letters we get an inside view of the movement, which became Christianity. In these letters we see Jesus being thrust into the place of a political leader and in turned killed by the Romans and Jewish leaders. The inside view shows us that no one actually thought he was anything but an inconvenience to the established leadership, which had determined to have him killed to protect their positions. The political uprising crucifixion fit into what the Jewish people were expecting from their messiah. But the question remains. Did they expect this and thus cause it to happen?

There is very little unbiased information about Jesus. The problem in understanding Jesus from a historical perspective begins with the fact that we have rather limited sources for reconstructing his life. Those sources are primarily the gospel traditions that we have in the New Testament, some apocryphal materials from the early Christian tradition, and some sources external to the New Testament. Some sources external to the Bible are more biased than others. For example, we can argue that historians, such as Josephus, are not biased, but that would overlook the fact that he was a Pharisee who was captured by Romans and persuaded to join them under threat of death. Josephus may have been a bit biased. Other sources, such as

71

Gnostic gospels have a theological agenda, just as orthodox scripture has its agenda to maintain a particular view. One must ask what or who the source is and what may their biases and agendas be. There are very few, if any, that lack social biases or political / religious agendas. Let us examine Josephus a little closer to expand this point.

Josephus, the Jewish historian, wrote at the end of the first century. In book 18 of his "Antiquities of the Jews," there is a small passage about Jesus. He also reports about John the Baptist, and about James, the brother of Jesus. His passages constitute the first external testimonies to the existence of Jesus by someone who was not a follower. Most historians believe that external sources, like Josephus, don't have the same biases of faith or hate seen in other sources, including the gospels, so independent sources, like Josephus, may paint a clearer picture. At first blush this seems a valid point but one must also ask who and what the historian himself may be. Josephus was not all that unbiased. He may have attempted to call things as he saw them but one cannot be totally removed from cultural myopathy, not even Josephus, who as it turns out was a Pharisee.

Josephus was born into a Jewish family around 37 AD. He was a well-studied and intelligent man and became a Pharisee. He was a member of a group of zealots who rebelled against Roman rule between 66 and 74 AD. For a time he was the leader of their forces in Galilee and was part of the battles leading to the Roman destruction of Jerusalem in AD 70. He was captured by the Romans, and would have been executed, but he became a traitor to his first cause and joined the Romans. His intellect and political savvy were rewarded by the Romans, being traits they admired and Josephus was promoted accordingly. Josephus became the Roman emperor's adviser on Jewish affairs, and died in about 98 AD.

Josephus took the Roman name, 'Flavius', in honor of the Roman man who sponsored or "guaranteed" his talents and his allegiance to the emperor. His book 'Jewish War' focused on the period AD 66 to 73 and was based on his first-hand experiences and interviews. 'Antiquities of the Jews' covers the whole of Jewish history up to AD 66.

In his writings, Josephus mentions the Pharisees, the Sadducees, the Essenes, and the Herodians. He mentions Caiaphas, Pontius Pilate, John the Baptist, Jesus (twice) and James the brother of Jesus. The Essenes were a strict religious sect within Judaism who founded the Qumran community, where the Dead Sea Scrolls were found. Josephus spent time with the Essenes. This is how he describes it according to Carsten Peter Thiede in 'The Dead Sea Scrolls and the Jewish origins of Christianity":

When I was about sixteen, I wanted to gain first-hand experience of our different movements. There are three: first, the Pharisees, second the Sadducees, and third the Essenes - as I have noted frequently. I thought I would be able to choose the best, by learning about all these schools. Thus I steeled myself for the task and studied the three courses with some effort.

In book 18 of the Antiquities, 63-64, the text of Josephus as we have it today says:

About this time there lived Jesus, a wise man, if indeed it is lawful to call him a man, for he was a performer of wonderful deeds, a teacher of such men as are happy to accept the truth. He won over many of the Jews and many of the Gentiles. He was the Christ, and when Pilate, at the suggestion of the leading men among us, had condemned him to the cross, those who had loved him at the first did not forsake him; for he appeared to them alive again on the third day, as the prophets of God had foretold these and ten thousand other wonders about him. And the tribe of Christians, so named from him, are not extinct to this day.'

The comment about it being "lawful" to call Jesus a man is not something that a Pharisee or Roman adviser would write. Most scholars today agree that the text had been altered by early Christians.

The original rendering may be closer to:

At this time there appeared Jesus, a wise man. For he was a doer of startling (controversial) deeds, a teacher of people who receive the truth with pleasure. And he gained a following among many Jews and among many of Gentile origin. And when Pilate, because of an accusation made by the leading men among us, condemned him to the cross, those who had loved him previously did not cease to do so. And up until this very day the tribe of Christians (named after him) had not died out.

(per Meier, op. cit., page 61).

There is a second reference to Jesus in the works of Josephus. In Antiquities 20.200, Josephus writes that in 62 CE the high priest Ananus was deposed because he had illegally convened the Sanhedrin in order to condemn James, the brother of Jesus, and some other men, whom he accused of having broken the law. They were handed over to be stoned.

Josephus, a Pharisee and now a Roman, could not speak admiringly of Jesus, even though Jesus had died before Josephus, or he would risk being stripped and divested of both privilege and property, and maybe even life. Josephus had already proven himself to be politically and morally malleable. It does not seem reasonable to think these words are actually his.

Here, I must say that just because the comments from Josephus may or may not be authentic, it does not disprove the existence of Jesus. Most credible historians believe Jesus existed. I use Josephus and the arguments about the references to Jesus to show how difficult it is to sift fact from embellishment.

Many historians believe the paragraph on Jesus was added to Josephus's work at the beginning of the 4th century, during Constantine's reign, probably by or under the order of Bishop Eusebius, who proclaimed that it was permissible for Christians to lie in order to further the Kingdom of God. He justified his lies by pointing to the New Testament, where Paul writes in the 3rd Chapter of Romans: "For if the truth of God hath more abounded through my lie unto his glory, why yet am I also judged as a sinner?"

Owing to our doubt, let us look at what some modern historians think of these passages.

"Josephus, the renowned Jewish historian, was a native of Judea. He was born in 37 A. D., and was a contemporary of the Apostles. He was, for a time, Governor of Galilee, the province in which Christ lived and taught. He traversed every part of this province and visited the places where but a generation before Christ had performed his prodigies. He resided in Cana, the very city in which Christ is said to have wrought his first miracle. He mentions every noted personage of Palestine and describes every important event which occurred there during the first seventy years of the Christian era. But Christ was of too little consequence and his deeds too trivial to merit a line from this historian's pen." (Remsberg, Ibid.)

John E. Remsberg, The Christ

Late in the first century Josephus wrote his celebrated work, "The Antiquities of the Jews," giving a history of his race from the earliest ages down to his own time. Modern versions of this work contain the following passage:

"Now, there was about this time Jesus, a wise man, if it be lawful to call him a man, for he was a doer of wonderful works; a teacher of such men as receive the truth with pleasure. He drew over to him both many of the Jews, and many of the Gentiles. He was [the] Christ; and when Pilate, at the suggestion of the principal men amongst us, had condemned him to the cross, those that loved him at the first did not forsake him; for he appeared to them alive again the third day, as the divine prophets had foretold these and ten thousand other wonderful things concerning him; and the tribe of Christians, so named from him, are not extinct at this day" (Book IXVIII, Chap. iii, sec. 3).

For nearly sixteen hundred years Christians have been citing this passage as a testimonial, not merely to the historical existence, but to the divine character of Jesus Christ. And yet a ranker forgery was never penned.

Its language is Christian. Every line proclaims it the work of a Christian writer. "If it be lawful to call him a man." "He was the Christ." "He appeared to them alive again the third day, as the divine prophets had foretold these and ten thousand other wonderful things concerning, him." These are the words of a Christian, a believer in the divinity of Christ. Josephus was a Jew, a devout believer in the Jewish faith -- the last man in the world to acknowledge the divinity of Christ. The inconsistency of this evidence was early recognized, and Ambrose, writing in the generation succeeding its first appearance (360 A. D.) offers the following explanation, which only a theologian could frame: "If the Jews do not believe us, let them, at least, believe their own writers. Josephus, whom they esteem a very great man, hath said this, and yet hath he spoken truth after such a manner; and so far was his mind wandered from the right way, that even he was not a believer as to what he himself said; but thus he spake, in order to deliver historical truth, because he thought it not lawful for him to deceive, while yet he was no believer, because of the hardness of his heart, and his perfidious intention."

Its brevity disproves its authenticity. Josephus' work is voluminous and exhaustive. It comprises twenty books. Whole pages are devoted to petty robbers and obscure seditious leaders. Nearly forty chapters are devoted to the life of a single king. Yet this remarkable being, the greatest product of his race, a being of whom the prophets foretold ten thousand wonderful things, a being greater than any earthly king, is dismissed with a dozen lines.

It interrupts the narrative. Section 2 of the chapter containing it gives an account of a Jewish sedition which was suppressed by Pilate with great slaughter. The account ends as follows: "There were a great number of them slain by this means, and others of them ran away wounded; and thus an end was put to this sedition." Section 4, as now numbered, begins with these words: "About the same time also another sad calamity put the Jews into disorder." The one section naturally and logically follows the other. Yet between these two closely connected paragraphs the one relating to Christ is placed; thus making the words, "another sad calamity," refer to the advent of this wise and wonderful being. The early Christian fathers were not acquainted with it. Justin Martyr, Tertullian, Clement of Alexandria, and Origen all would have quoted this passage had it existed in their time. The failure of even one of these fathers to notice it would be sufficient to throw doubt upon its genuineness; the failure of all of them to notice it proves conclusively that it is spurious, that it was not in existence during the second and third centuries.

As this passage first appeared in the writings of the ecclesiastical historian, Eusebius, as this author openly advocated the use of fraud and deception in furthering the interests of the church, as he is known to have mutilated and perverted the text of Josephus in other instances, and as the manner of its presentation is calculated to excite suspicion, the forgery has generally been charged to him. In his "Evangelical Demonstration," written early in the fourth century, after citing all the known evidences of Christianity, he thus introduces the Jewish historian: "Certainly the attestations I have already produced concerning our Savior may be sufficient. However, it may not be amiss if, over and above, we make use of Josephus the Jew for a further witness" (Book III, p. 124).

Chrysostom and Photius both reject this passage. Chrysostom, a reader of Josephus, who preached and wrote in the latter part of the fourth century, in his defense of Christianity, needed this evidence, but was too honest or too wise to use it. Photius, who made a revision of Josephus, writing five hundred years after the time of Eusebius, ignores the passage, and admits that Josephus has made no mention of Christ. Modern Christian scholars generally concede that the passage is a forgery. Dr. Lardner, one of the ablest defenders of Christianity, adduces the following arguments against its genuineness: "I do not perceive that we at all want the suspected testimony to Jesus, which was never quoted by any of our Christian ancestors before Eusebius. Nor do I recollect that Josephus has anywhere mentioned the name or word Christ, in any of his works; except the testimony above mentioned, and the passage concerning James, the Lord's brother. It interrupts the narrative. The language is quite Christian. It is not quoted by Chrysostom, though he often refers to Josephus, and could not have omitted quoting it had it been then in the text. It is not quoted by Photius, though he has three articles concerning Josephus. Under the article Justus of Tiberias, this author (Photius) expressly states that the historian [Josephus], being a Jew, has not taken the least notice of Christ. Neither Justin in his dialogue with Trypho the Jew, nor Clemens Alexandrinus, who made so many extracts from ancient authors, nor Origen against Celsus, has ever mentioned this testimony. But, on the contrary, in chapter xxxv of the first book of that work, Origen openly affirms that Josephus, who had mentioned

John the Baptist, did not acknowledge Christ" (Answer to Dr. Chandler).

Again Dr. Lardner says: "This passage is not quoted nor referred to by any Christian writer before Eusebius, who flourished at the beginning of the fourth century. If it had been originally in the works of Josephus it would have been highly proper to produce it in their disputes with Jews and Gentiles. But it is never quoted by Justin Martyr, or Clement of Alexandria, nor by Tertullian or Origen, men of great learning, and well acquainted with the works of Josephus. It was certainly very proper to urge it against the Jews. It might also have been fitly urged against the Gentiles. A testimony so favorable to Jesus in the works of Josephus, who lived so soon after our Savior, who was so well acquainted with the transactions of his own country, who had received so many favors from Vespasian and Titus, would not be overlooked or neglected by any Christian apologist" (Lardner's Works, vol.I, chap. iv).

Bishop Warburton declares it to be a forgery: "If a Jew owned the truth of Christianity, he must needs embrace it. We, therefore, certainly conclude that the paragraph where Josephus, who was as much a Jew as the religion of Moses could make him, is made to acknowledge Jesus as the Christ, in terms as strong as words could do it, is a rank forgery, and a very stupid one, too" (Quoted by Lardner, Works, Vol. I, chap. iv).

The Rev. Dr. Giles, of the Established Church of England, says: "Those who are best acquainted with the character of Josephus, and the style of his writings, have no hesitation in condemning this passage as a forgery, interpolated in the text during the third century by some pious Christian, who was scandalized that so famous a writer as Josephus should have taken no notice of the gospels, or of Christ, their subject. But the zeal of the interpolator has outrun his discretion, for we might as well expect to gather grapes from thorns, or figs from thistles, as to find this notice of Christ among the Judaizing writings of Josephus. It is well known that this author was a zealous Jew, devoted to the laws of Moses and the traditions of his countrymen. How, then, could he have written that Jesus was the Christ? Such an admission would have proved him to be a Christian himself, in which case the passage under consideration, too long for a Jew, would have been far too short for a believer in the new religion, and thus the passage stands forth, like an ill-set jewel, contrasting most inharmoniously with everything around it. If it had been genuine, we might be sure that Justin Martyr, Tertullian, and Chrysostom would have quoted it in their controversies with the Jews, and that Origen or Photius would have mentioned it. But Eusebius, the ecclesiastical historian (I, ii), is the first who quotes it, and our reliance on the judgment or even honesty of this writer is not so great as to allow our considering everything found in his works as undoubtedly genuine" (Christian Records, p. 30).

The Rev. S. Baring-Gould, in his "Lost and Hostile Gospels," says: "This passage is first quoted by Eusebius (fl. A. D. 315) in two places (Hist. Eccl., lib. i, c. xi ; Demonst. Evang., lib. iii); but it was unknown to Justin Martyr (A. D. 140) Clement of Alexandria (A. D. 192), Tertullian (A. D. 193) and Origen (A. D. 230). Such a testimony would certainly have been produced by Justin in his apology or in his controversy with Trypho the Jew, had it existed in the copies of Josephus at his time. The silence of Origen is still more significant. Celsus, in his book against Christianity, introduces a Jew. Origen attacks the argument of Celsus and his Jew. He could not have failed to quote the words of Josephus, whose writings he knew, had the passage existed in the genuine text. He, indeed, distinctly affirms that Josephus did not believe in Christ (Contr. Cels. i)."

Dr. Chalmers ignores it, and admits that Josephus is silent regarding Christ. He says: "The entire silence of Josephus upon the subject of Christianity, though he wrote after the destruction of Jerusalem, and gives us the history of that period in which Christ and his Apostles lived, is certainly a very striking circumstance" (Kneeland's Review, p. 169).

Canon Farrar, who has written the Christian life of Christ, says: "The single passage in which he [Josephus] alludes to him is interpolated, if not wholly spurious" (Life of Christ, Vol. I, p. 46). The following, from Dr. Farrar's pen, is to be found in the "Encyclopedia Britannica": "That Josephus wrote the whole passage as it now stands no sane critic can believe." "There are, however, two reasons which are alone sufficient to prove that the whole passage is spurious -- one that it was unknown to Origen and the earlier fathers, and the other that its place in the text is uncertain." (Ibid) The Rev. Dr. Hooykaas, of Holland, says: "Flavius Josephus, the well known historian of the Jewish people, was born in A. D. 37, only two years after the death of Jesus; but though his work is of inestimable value as our chief authority for the circumstances of the times in which Jesus and his Apostles came forward, yet he does not seem to have mentioned Jesus himself. At any rate, the passage in his "Jewish Antiquities" that refers to him is certainly spurious, and was inserted by a later and a Christian hand." (Bible for Learners, Vol. III, p. 27) This conclusion of Dr. Hooykaas is endorsed by the eminent Dutch critic, Dr. Kuenen.

Dr. Alexander Campbell, one of America's ablest Christian apologists, says: "Josephus, the Jewish historian, was contemporary with the Apostles, having been born in the year 37. From his situation and habits, he had every access to know all that took place at the rise of the Christian religion. Respecting the founder of this religion, Josephus has thought fit to be silent in history. The present copies of his work contain one passage which speaks very respectfully of Jesus Christ, and ascribes to him the character of the Messiah. But as Josephus did not embrace Christianity, and as this passage is not quoted or referred to until the beginning of the fourth century, it is, for these and other reasons, generally accounted spurious" (Evidences of Christianity, from Campbell-Owen Debate, p. 312)

But, like a snake turning on itself, if we take into consideration other sources and the consistency of these sources we may say that even if the text of Josephus was changed it was likely not completely forged. Indeed, having removed the Christian embellishment from his text it comes totally in line with other comments by various historians of ancient times. Yes, there was a historical Jesus. His existence is proven by the preponderance of coordinated evidence.

If we take the references in the works of Josephus as fact they tell us the following about Jesus:

He was a historical figure and thus real.

He was a Jewish man.

He was born in Bethlehem but hailed from Nazareth.

He was a teacher.

He did things that were startling.

There were claims that Jesus was the Messiah (that is, the Christ).

He gathered a band of followers, who continued to follow him after his death.

He had a brother called James.

James was executed in AD 62 with the consent of Pilot at the urging of the Jewish leaders.

Other evidence of the existence of Jesus can be extracted from historians living around the time of Jesus, but, (and this a large caveat), there are few if any that lived at the exact time of Jesus and thus they report on what had been said or written about Jesus and not what they actually encountered first person.

CORNELIUS TACITUS (55 - 120 A.D.) Tacitus was a 1st and 2nd century Roman and is considered one of the greatest historians of ancient Rome. Tacitus verifies the Biblical account of Jesus' execution at the hands of Pontius Pilate who governed Judea from 26-36 A.D. during the reign of Tiberius.

"Christus, the founder of the [Christian] name, was put to death by Pontius Pilate, procurator of Judea in the reign of Tiberius. But the pernicious superstition, repressed for a time, broke out again, not only through Judea, where the mischief originated through the city of Rome also." Annals XV, 44

GAIUS SUETONIUS TRANQUILLUS (69 - 130 A.D.) Suetonius was a prominent Roman historian who recorded the lives of the Roman Caesars and the historical events surrounding their reigns. He served as a court official under Hadrian in the Imperial House. Suetonius records plight of Christians mentioned in Acts 18:2 and names the founder of the sect of Jews.

"As the Jews were making constant disturbances at the instigation of Chrestus (Christ), Claudius expelled them from Rome." Life of Claudius 25.4

(Because Chrestus was an actual Greek name, critics speculate Suetonius may have been referring to a specific civil agitator. It was common for both pagan and Christian authors to spell the name using either an e or an i

PLINY THE YOUNGER (63 - 113 A.D) Pliny the Younger writes of torturing and executing Christians who refused to deny Christ. Those who denied the charges were spared and ordered to exalt the Roman gods and curse the name of Christ. Pliny complains to Emperor Trajan that too many were refusing to deny Christ and were being killed.

"I asked them directly if they were Christians...those who persisted, I ordered away... Those who denied they were or ever had been Christians...worshiped both your image and the images of the gods and cursed Christ. They used to gather on a stated day before dawn and sing to Christ as if he were a god... All the more I believed it necessary to find out what was the truth from two servant maids, which were called deaconesses, by means of torture. Nothing more did I find than a disgusting, fanatical superstition. Therefore I stopped the examination, and hastened to consult you...on account of the number of people endangered. For many of all ages, all classes, and both sexes already are brought into danger..." Pliny's letter to Emperor Trajan

CELSUS (~ 178 A.D.) Celsus was a second century Roman author and avid opponent of Christianity. He went to great lengths to disprove the divinity of Jesus yet never denied His actual existence. Celsus is not actually arguing the existence of Jesus as much as he is denying the truth of the religion that has sprung up around Jesus. He only assumes Jesus existed based on the fact that so many follow the Christian sect so blindly. Yet, this is neither proof of Jesus nor the legitimacy of the faith. Millions have died for a lie they believed in. Religious and political wars abound with their bodies.

Celsus wrote:

On Jesus' Miracles: "Jesus, on account of his poverty, was hired out to go to Egypt. While there he acquired certain [magical] powers... He returned home highly elated at possessing these powers, and on the strength of them gave himself out to be a god... It was by means of sorcery that He was able to accomplish the wonders which He performed... Let us believe that these cures, or the resurrection, or the feeding of a multitude with a few loaves... These are nothing more than the tricks of jugglers... It is by the names of certain demons, and by the use of
incantations, that the Christians appear to be possessed of [miraculous] power..."

On the Virgin Birth: "Jesus had come from a village in Judea, and was the son of a poor Jewess who gained her living by the work of her hands. His mother had been turned out by her husband, who was a carpenter by trade, on being convicted of adultery with a Roman soldier named Panthera. Being thus driven away by her husband, and wandering about in disgrace, she gave birth to Jesus, a bastard."

(The Talmud which makes the same accusation. This gives us reason to believe Celsus might have referenced Jewish sources for some of his arguments.)

MARA BAR-SERAPION (Post 70 A.D) Mara Bar-Serapion of Syria penned this letter from prison to his son.

"What advantage did the Athenians gain from putting Socrates to death? Famine and plague came upon them as a judgment for their crime. What advantage did the men of Samos gain from burning Pythagoras? In a moment their land was covered with sand. What advantage did the Jews gain from executing their wise King? It was just after that their kingdom was abolished. God justly avenged these three wise men: The Athenians died of hunger. The Samians were overwhelmed by the sea. The Jews, ruined and driven from their land, live in complete
dispersion. But Socrates did not die for good. He lived on in the teachings of Plato. Pythagoras did not die for good. He lived on in the statue of Hera. Nor did the wise King die for good. He lived on in the teaching which He had given."

It is acknowledged that the above passage has no name but instead simply the title of "Wise King" and thus may not refer to Jesus at all. If it weren't for the fact that the timing and circumstances give reason to believe that the writer refers to Jesus.

THE BABYLONIAN TALMUD The Babylonian Talmud is an ancient record of Jewish history, laws, and rabbinic teachings compiled throughout the centuries. Though it does not accept the divinity of Jesus, it confirms the belief He was hanged (an idiom for crucifixion) on the eve of the Passover.

"On the eve of the Passover Yeshu (Jesus) [Some texts: Yeshu the Nazarene] was hanged [crucified]. Forty days before the execution, a herald went forth and cried, 'He is going forth to be stoned because he has practiced sorcery and enticed Israel to apostasy. Any one who can say anything in his favor, let him come forward and plead on his behalf.' But since nothing was brought forward in his favor he was hanged on the eve of the Passover."

This is what some historians wrote about Jesus. None of them lived in his time. It is likely that Jesus was just a footnote at the time. He was a man going around preaching in a very politically charged environment, as were many others who had gained a following and were being watched. Around his time there were several men named Jesus doing the same thing. It was a common name.

The name, Jesus embodied the hope of the Jewish people, who were kept as second class citizens under the boot of Rome. Jesus means in Hebrew: "God saves." According to Catholic teaching, at the annunciation, the angel Gabriel gave him the name Jesus as his proper name, which expressed both his identity and his mission.

The name "Jesus" is the Greek expression of the Hebrew name, "Joshua." Both Joshua and Jesus are actually anglicized renditions of the what is closer to the name Yeshua. The first letter in the name Yeshua ("Jesus") is the yod. Yod represents the "Y" sound in Hebrew. Many names in the Bible that begin with yod are mispronounced by English speakers because the yod in these names was transliterated in English Bibles with the letter "J" rather than "Y". This came about because in early English the letter "J" was pronounced the way we pronounce "Y" today.

Iesous is the Greek transliteration of the Hebrew name Yeshua, and its English spelling is "Jesus."

In the Jewish world of the time the name Yeshua was one of the most common names because it embodied the hope of the people that God would send someone to free them from Roman tyranny.

Other Men Named Jesus

Jesus ben Sirach was the author of the Book of Sirach (aka 'Ecclesiasticus, or the Wisdom of Jesus the Son of Sirach'), part of Old Testament Apocrypha. Ben Sirach, writing in Greek about 180 BC, brought together Jewish 'wisdom' and Homeric-style heroes.

Jesus ben Pandira was reported to have been a prophet and was said to have done miracles during the reign of Alexander Jannaeus (106-79 BC), one of the most ruthless of the Maccabean kings. His end-time prophecy and agitation upset the king. He met his own premature end-time by being hung on a tree – and on the eve of a Passover. Scholars have speculated this Jesus founded the Essene sect.

Jesus ben Ananias. Beginning in 62 AD he began to preach in Jerusalem. We have some of his prophecies, thanks to Josephus. "A voice from the east, a voice from the west, a voice from the four winds, a voice against Jerusalem and the holy house, a voice against the bridegrooms and the brides, and a voice against the whole people."
– Josephus, Wars 6.3.
He was arrested and flogged by the Romans, then released. He died during the siege of Jerusalem from a rock hurled by a Roman catapult.

Jesus ben Saphat. In the insurrection of 68 AD in Galilee, he led the rebels in Tiberias ("the leader of a seditious tumult of mariners and poor people" – Josephus, Life 12.66). When the city was about to fall to Vespasian's legionaries he fled north to Tarichea on the Sea of Galilee.

Jesus ben Gamala. During 68/69 AD he attempted to make peace and quiet the civil war wrecking Judaea. He tried to have peace talks with the besieging Idumeans, led by James and John, sons of Susa. Nonetheless, when the Idumeans breached the walls he was put to death and his body thrown to the dogs.

Jesus ben Thebuth was a priest in 69 AD, who saved his own life by betraying the Jews and surrendering the treasures of the Temple, which included two holy candlesticks, goblets of pure gold, sacred curtains and robes of the high priests. The booty figured prominently in the Triumph held for Vespasian and his son Titus.

Jesus was a common name and many men named Jesus were religious and political leaders. Some were beaten and some were crucified. It is possible that the Jesus of the Bible is a composite of some of these, as storied are combined and embellished in time. This does not mean that there was not a Jesus of Nazareth. It simply means there were many other Jesus' and they had their stories also.

What did Jesus Look Like?

It must be said from the onset that the authenticity of the following letters is in question. They should be weighted accordingly.

The following was taken from a manuscript in the possession of Lord Kelly, and in his library, and was copied from an original letter of **Publius Lentullus** at Rome. It being the usual custom of Roman Governors to advertise the Senate and people of such material things as happened in their provinces in the days of Tiberius Caesar, Publius Lentullus, President of Judea, wrote the following epistle (letter) to the Senate concerning the Nazarene called Jesus.

"There appeared in these our days a man, of the Jewish Nation, of great virtue, named Yeshua [Jesus], who is yet living among us, and of the Gentiles is accepted for a Prophet of truth, but His own disciples call Him the Son of God- He raiseth the dead and cureth all manner of diseases. A man of stature somewhat tall, and comely, with very reverent countenance, such as the beholders may both love and fear, his hair of (the colour of) the chestnut, full ripe, plain to His ears, whence downwards it is more orient and curling and wavering about His shoulders. In the midst of His head is a seam or partition in His hair, after the manner of the Nazarenes. His forehead plain and very delicate; His face without spot or wrinkle, beautified with a lovely red; His nose and mouth so formed as nothing can be reprehended;

His beard thickish, in colour like His hair, not very long, but forked; His look innocent and mature; His eyes grey, clear, and quick- In reproving hypocrisy He is terrible; in admonishing, courteous and fair spoken; pleasant in conversation, mixed with gravity. It cannot be remembered that any have seen Him Laugh, but many have seen Him Weep. In proportion of body, most excellent; His hands and arms delicate to behold. In speaking, very temperate, modest, and wise. A man, for His singular beauty, surpassing the children of men"

The letter from Pontius Pilate to Tiberius Caesar

This is a reprinting of a letter from Pontius Pilate to Tiberius Caesar describing the physical appearance of Jesus. Copies are in the Congressional Library in Washington, D.C.

TO TIBERIUS CAESAR:

A young man appeared in Galilee preaching with humble unction, a new law in the Name of the God that had sent Him. At first I was apprehensive that His design was to stir up the people against the Romans, but my fears were soon dispelled. Jesus of Nazareth spoke rather as a friend of the Romans than of the Jews. One day I observed in the midst of a group of people a young man who was leaning against a tree, calmly addressing the multitude. I was told it was Jesus. This I could easily have suspected so great was the difference between Him and those who were listening to Him. His golden colored hair and beard gave to his appearance a celestial aspect. He appeared to be about 30 years of age. Never have I seen a sweeter or more serene countenance. What a contrast between Him and His bearers with their black beards and tawny complexions! Unwilling to interrupt Him by my presence, I continued my walk but signified to my secretary to join the group and listen. Later, my secretary reported that never had he seen in the works of all the philosophers anything that compared to the teachings of Jesus. He told me that Jesus was neither seditious nor rebellious, so we extended to Him our protection. He was at liberty to act, to speak, to assemble and to address the people. This unlimited freedom provoked the Jews -- not the poor but the rich and powerful.

Later, I wrote to Jesus requesting an interview with Him at the Praetorium. He came. When the Nazarene made His appearance I was having my morning walk and as I faced Him my feet seemed fastened with an iron hand to the marble pavement and I trembled in every limb as a guilty culprit, though he was calm. For some time I stood admiring this extraordinary Man. There was nothing in Him that was repelling, nor in His character, yet I felt awed in His presence. I told Him that there was a magnetic simplicity about Him and His personality that elevated Him far above the philosophers and teachers of His day.

Now, Noble Sovereign, these are the facts concerning Jesus of Nazareth and I have taken the time to write you in detail concerning these matters. I say that such a man who could convert water into wine, change death into life, disease into health; calm the stormy seas, is not guilty of any criminal offense and as others have said, we must agree -- truly this is the Son of God.

Your most obedient servant,
Pontius Pilate

Another description of Jesus is found in **"The Archko Volume"** which contains official court documents from the days of Jesus. This information substantiates that He came from a genetic line which had blue eyes and golden hair. In a chapter entitled "Gamaliel's Interview" it states concerning Jesus (Yeshua) appearance:

"I asked him to describe this person to me, so that I might know him if I should meet him. He said: 'If you ever meet him [Yeshua] you will know him. While he is nothing but a man, there is something about him that distinguishes him from every other man. He is the picture of his mother, only he has not her smooth, round face. His hair is a little more golden than hers, though it is as much from sunburn as anything else. He is tall, and his shoulders are a little drooped; his visage is thin and of a swarthy complexion, though this is from exposure. His eyes are large and a soft blue, and rather dull and heavy....' This Jew [Nazarite] is convinced that he is the Messiah of the world. ...this was the same person that was born of the virgin in Bethlehem some twenty-six years before..."

- The Archko Volume, translated by Drs. McIntosh and Twyman of the Antiquarian Lodge, Genoa, Italy, from manuscripts in Constantinople and the records of the Senatorial Docket taken from the Vatican of Rome (1896) 92-93

The Language of Jesus

The language of love, engagement, and marriage is used in the Bible to illustrate the place of Jesus in our lives. Throughout his ministry Jesus uses marriage and betrothal to make points regarding our relationship with God, himself, and each other. He is drawing an analogy from Jewish marriage customs in his time, which may be lost on the modern reader. An overview of the process of betrothal and wedding will be presented but before we cover the ceremony we must ask one overarching question. Did Jesus and the apostles use language and metaphor regarding love and marriage so extensively in their teachings and yet they knew nothing about it on a personal level? It seems if Jesus did this he would be looked upon by the masses he was addressing as less than credible.

There were several steps in ancient times for a couple to progress from meeting to marriage. The first major step in a Jewish marriage was betrothal. Betrothal involved the establishment of a marriage covenant. By Jesus' time it was usual for such a covenant to be established as the result of the prospective bridegroom taking the initiative. Betrothal was what we would consider an "engagement" today. The first stage of the betrothal was finding a suitable spouse for the bride or bridegroom. In the ancient Near Eastern culture the families of the bride and groom most often initiated the search. The man and woman were pledged to each other at ages as young as twelve or thirteen.

Before witnesses, the couple entered into betrothal by way of a public promise. The society at the time gave the female to the male. Once a couple entered this stage of betrothal, it could only be broken by a formal divorce. The terms "husband" and "wife" were used during this period, though the couple did not live together, however adultery was punishable by stoning. Also, if one of the young people died, the other would be considered a "widow" or "widower".

The length of betrothal was generally about a year. This period of separation afforded the bride time to gather her trousseau and to prepare for married life. The groom occupied himself with the preparation of living accommodations in his father's house to which he could bring his bride.

The wedding was a special ceremony. Both bride and bridegroom wore special wedding clothes.

The wedding started with a procession from the home of the groom. The prospective bridegroom would travel from his father's house to the home of the prospective bride. He and his companions began a procession to the bride's home. It was a joyous occasion since the bride did not know the exact time of the arrival. The companions announced "The Bridegroom Cometh!" There he would negotiate with the father of the young woman to determine the price (mohar) that he must pay to purchase his bride. Once the bridegroom paid the purchase price, the marriage covenant was thereby established, and the young man and woman were regarded to be husband and wife. From that moment on the bride was declared to be consecrated or sanctified, set apart exclusively for her bridegroom. The company would then escort the bride and her companions back to the groom's home where there would be a special supper prepared. During this celebration, the parents and friends blessed the couple and the father of the bride drew up a written marriage contract. As a symbol of the covenant relationship that had been established, the groom and bride would drink from a cup of wine over which a betrothal benediction had been pronounced. The couple would then be escorted to a special "bridal chamber" where the marriage would be consummated.

Prior to entering the chamber the bride remained veiled so that no one could see her face. While the groomsmen and bridesmaids would wait outside, the bride and groom would enter the bridal chamber alone. There in the privacy of that place they would enter into physical union for the first time, thereby consummating the marriage that had been covenanted earlier.

As prescribed in the Old Testament, evidence of the bride's virginity would then be given. Marriage festivities continued for up to a week.

It was in this period of time within a wedding of friends that Jesus did his first miracle. He turned water to wine so that festivities could continue. He had reverence and was joyous in the event. If he preached celibacy he would not have been there.

During the seven days of the wedding festivities the bride remained hidden in the bridal chamber. At the conclusion of these seven days the groom would bring his bride out of the bridal chamber, now with her veil removed, so that all could see who his bride was.

Marriage was an important part of life in the time of Jesus. He was a celebrated part of at least one such ceremony. It was important enough to him that he performed his first miracle at a wedding. Jesus loved his own family. He reverenced his mother. His last act on earth was to make sure she was cared for. Although this is not concrete proof the Jesus was married, it is proof that Jesus supported the family unit and attended marriage ceremonies. As a celibate male it is not likely he would have been asked to attend or would have done so. It would have been contrary to social norms.

Could Jesus have been invited to the wedding even though he was celibate and rejected marriage for himself. Absolutely, but it would have been awkward.

What We Know Thus Far

Jesus was born in Bethlehem but hailed from the town of Nazareth. His mother was Mary. Rumors say she got pregnant out of wedlock and Jesus was a bastard. Others say his birth was miraculous because Mary was a virgin. He was tall and thin. He had blue eyes and golden hair with undertones of red (chestnut). His hair was wavy and he wore it down to his shoulders and parted in the middle. His beard was thick and possibly grew a little forked at his chin. Jesus had a brother called James who was executed by the Jewish leaders in AD 62

Jesus was a modest, courteous man with a serene disposition. Although he did not laugh much he had a pleasant disposition. He was a teacher and his mannerisms attracted people. Some people said he did startling things, maybe even miracles. He gathered a band of followers, who continued to follow him after his death. Some of these people claimed Jesus was the Messiah.

At this point in time there were no claim of Jesus being God. There was no thought of the trinity. There was no discussion of the rapture. Jesus was thought to have been anointed or appointed by God, because of his pure heart, to lead people back into a communion with God. As Messiah Jesus was expected to stand against Roman rule and free the Jewish people, uniting all people under the authority of God and the Torah. His leadership would have stripped the Sanhedrin of its power, since Jesus would become king. It would also destroy Rome's control. The Romans and Jewish leaders knew this and so they killed him. Jesus himself never made these claims nor did he preach war or sedition. It was what his followers claimed that pushed him to his death. Pilot was the person who was responsible for the final decision regarding the crucifixion of Jesus.

Recap of Details

Jesus was a historical figure and thus real.

He was a Jewish man.

He was born in Bethlehem but hailed from Nazareth.

He was tall.

He was thin.

He had drooped shoulders.

He had golden-brown hair with red undertones.

He had a pleasant disposition but seldom laughed.

He was calm.

His mannerisms and personality were pleasant.

He was a teacher.

He did things that were startling.

There were claims that Jesus was the Messiah (that is, the Christ).

He gathered a band of followers, who continued to follow him after his death.

He had a brother called James.

James was executed by in AD 62 with the consent of Pilot at the urging of the Jewish leaders.

That is actually quite a bit of detail, when all sources are allowed to speak. But are these sources reliable enough to be counted as evidence? You will have to decide.

Outside of documents presented here, and a few others, all of which the church dismisses as "not authentic," there are no "eyewitness" accounts written about Jesus during his lifetime, so historians have to rely on interpretations of the four main canonical gospel texts, which were written decades after his death; possibly after a reinterpretation of his life and its meaning based on their view of Old Testament scripture. Untangling the man from the myth is a delicate undertaking, which is bound to fascinate some and offend others, but it should be of interest to all.

Tobias Hagerland, a doctoral candidate at the University of Gothenburg, Sweden said, "I think it's natural for human beings to ask questions 'why' something happened, and those are not exactly the questions dealt with in the Gospels," said Hagerland. "It could be of interest both to Christian believers and to critics of that religion to know which aspects of Christianity are rooted in historical facts and which are derived from religious convictions and experiences that cannot really be evaluated from an historical point of view."

Jesus is not a total mystery. The "Jesus" of history isn't a complete mystery to Biblical scholars, who often make a distinction between the man and the religious figure depicted in the scriptures.

"We do know some things about the historical Jesus — less than some Christians think, but more than some skeptics think. Though a few books have recently argued that Jesus never existed, the evidence that he did is persuasive to the vast majority of scholars, whether Christian or non-Christian," said Marcus Borg, a retired professor of religion and culture at Oregon State University and current fellow of the Jesus Seminar, a group of preeminent academics that debate the factuality of Jesus' life as portrayed in the Bible.

The following "facts" about Jesus would be affirmed by most history scholars, Borg said:

Jesus was born sometime just before 4 B.C. He grew up in Nazareth, a small village in Galilee, as part of the peasant class. Jesus' father was a carpenter and he became one, too, meaning that they had likely lost their agricultural land at some point.

Jesus was raised Jewish and he remained deeply Jewish all of his life. His intention was not to create a new religion. Rather, he saw himself as doing something within Judaism.

He left Nazareth as an adult, met the prophet John and was baptized by John. During his baptism, Jesus likely experienced some sort of divine vision.

Shortly afterwards, Jesus began his public preaching with the message that the world could be transformed into a "Kingdom of God."

He became a noted healer, teacher and prophet. More healing stories are told about Jesus than about any other figure in the Jewish tradition.

He was executed by Roman imperial authority.

His followers experienced him after his death. It is clear that they had visions of Jesus as they had known him during his historical life. Only after his death did they declare Jesus to be "Lord" or "the Son of God."

Some parts of the Bible likely strayed from history for emphasis, Hagerland agrees. The public's negative reaction to Jesus' preaching of forgiveness is one example, he said.

Without the reinterpretation of history in a metaphysical light, Jesus did not die for the sins of the world but rather was killed by those ruling that part of the world at the time. It was only after his death that his followers began to redefine the events in light of the Old Testament and thus assign meaning to events. It is much like seeing patterns in objects and events after the fact. Patterns are superimposed upon history and patterns are seen in retrospect as faces are seen in floor tiles and broken leaves.

Facts about the ancient Greco-Roman world can be overlooked or easily forgotten. Life did not have great meaning then, especially the life of a female. It must be stated clearly and without reservation that those who hold to the fact that Jesus was celibate may be completely correct seeing as how there was a deficit of females in that part of the world. The ratio of man to women was about 1.4 men to every woman. Why? Infanticide.

A first-century letter from a husband to his pregnant wife shows the contrast of his tender regard for his wife and hoped-for son, versus his disregard for a possible daughter: "I ask and beg of you to take good care of our baby son ... If you are delivered of a child [before I come home], if it is a boy, keep it; if a girl, discard it."

By the Law of Romulus in Rome, a father was required to raise all healthy male children, and only the firstborn female; any others were disposable. According to the Greek poet Posidippus (third century B.C.), "Everyone raises a son even if he is poor, but exposes a daughter even if he is rich."

However, this was Roman law and not Jewish custom. Widows were fined by Rome for out-living their husbands and being a drag on the economy. The Jewish custom as well as that of the early church, was to care for the widows and orphans. One of the last acts and requests by Jesus was to make sure his mother would be cared for after his death. Most intriguing is the clash of cultures at this time. Romans were killing their daughters and the ration of male to female was at 1.4 to 1. Meanwhile, in the Jewish population the custom of polygamy was still intact and the strength and leadership of women were being felt still.

The Place of Women in Society

History records the story of Babatha, who was a Jewish woman and a second wife. The record is interesting since it reveals much about the status of middle and upper class women of the time. It seems women were not the chattel we have been led to believe. Some Jewish women were very strong and influential beacons in their families and communities. We should not forget Deborah, the judge, and Phoebe, the deaconess. If you think these women were the exceptions you may be correct only in degree. History tells a story of what we take to be a common family, which could give pause and hopefully reconsideration of how autonomous and independent women could be.

In 1960, archeologist Yigael Yadin discovered a leather pouch containing personal documents of a women in a cave, which came to be known as the Cave of Letters, located near the Dead Sea. The documents found include such legal contracts concerning marriage, property transfers, and guardianship, ranging in dates from 96 to 134 AD. The documents depicted a vivid picture of life for a middle class to upper class Jewish woman during that time.

Babatha was born in approximately 104 CE in Maoza. She lived in the port town of Maoza in what is now modern day Jordan at beginning of the 2nd century CE. She was likely the only child since she inherited her father's date palm orchard upon her parents' deaths.

By 124 CE, she had been married and widowed with a young son, Jesus. The name, Jesus, was a very common name and more than one with that name was crucified. There was even more than one claiming to be the anointed one. Her son was not one of those. As far as we know he was an average child.

By 125 CE Babatha was remarried to Judah, owner of three date palm orchards in the town of Ein Gedi (an oasis and town situated west of the Dead Sea). Judah already had a wife. Judah's other wife had a teenage daughter. It is uncertain whether Babatha lived in the same home as the first wife or if Judah traveled between two separate households, as polygamy was still allowed in the Jewish community.

The documents found in the leather pouch offer information and insight concerning this marriage and her status in the relationship. In their marriage contract, Judah's debts become part of her liability, indicating a financial equality. In other words, Babatha was responsible for paying off her husband's debts if he were to die, become injured, or for some other reason could not pay.

In 128 CE, a legal document shows that Judah took a loan without interest from Babatha, showing that she had control of her own money despite the union. Now Judah was financially indebted to Babatha. Upon Judah's death in 130 CE, she seized his estates in Ein Gedi as a guarantee for payment against his debts, which she had covered through her loan to him, as stated in the marriage contract.

Another document of importance concerned the guardianship of Babatha's son. In 125 CE, Babatha brought a lawsuit to court against the appointed guardians of her orphaned son, citing their insufficient disbursement of funds. The document contains Babatha's petition that full guardianship responsibility of her son and his property be transferred to her control.

This is a huge insight into the range and depth of the place of Jewish women within marriages in the Jewish community at the time. We can assume it reflects marriage in general in that socio-economic class.

What is the lesson here regarding Jesus and Mary? Simply this;

Mary Magdalene was probably much like this woman. She was from a middle class or upper class family, capable of supporting the ministry of Jesus. She was self-determined. She had decided to be with Jesus and was helping him in his work. She supported his ministry and she loved Jesus.

The Manichaean Psalms is a manuscript discovered among other Coptic manuscripts in the Chester Beatty Collection, and translated into English the 1930's by Charles Allberry. The original text dates back to the last half of the 4th century. In the book is a psalm called the Psalms of Heracleides, Mary Magdalene is mentioned three times. Her devotion is summed up:

"Because she (Mary) has listened to her master she carried out his instructions with joy in her entire heart."

Who Was Mary Magdalene

As was customary in Bible times, the last name of the person was connected to his or her place of ancestry. This is evidenced in the fact that Jesus was called, "Jesus of Nazareth." Mary came from a town called Magdala, which was 120 miles north of Jerusalem on the shores of the Sea of Galilee. Magdala Tarichaea may have been the full name of the town. Magdala means tower, and Tarichaea means salted fish. The little village had the optimistic name of "The Tower of Salted Fish." The main business of the area was fishing and there is a good chance that Mary worked in the fish markets.

The Jewish text, "Lamentations Raba," mentions a town called "Magdala," and says Magdala was judged by God and destroyed because of its fornication. This could explain western Christianity's assumption that Mary Magdalene was the prostitute caught in adultery and presented to Jesus.

In fact, we have linked Mary Magdalene with many of the women in the New Testament who were redeemed or forgiven. This is a powerful and rich myth that resonates with both men and women who have fallen from grace and seek redemption. However, the Bible never says that Mary Magdalene was ever a prostitute.

The church rewrote the story of Mary Magdalene for their own purpose. In the gospels several women interact with Jesus and several of them were named Mary. There was Mary the mother of Jesus, Mary of Bethany, Mary the sister of Martha and Lazarus, Mary the mother of James and Joseph, and Mary the wife of Clopas.

There are three unnamed women who are identified as sinners. The is a woman with a soiled reputation, who in her throws of grief and repentance anoints Jesus' feet. There is a Samaritan woman who has been married many times but is now living with her boyfriend (a 21st century kind of person) whom Jesus meets at a well. There is an adulteress caught in the act whom Pharisees shove to the ground at the feet of Jesus as a test to see if he would keep the law and have her stoned to death. They were tired of his gospel of peace and forgiveness and wished to trap him.

Stories appear in some gospels and some stories are in multiple gospels but stories within the gospels vary, sometimes greatly from one another. The four Gospels are not eyewitness accounts but are memoirs written 35 to 65 years after Jesus' death. Matthew, Mark, and Luke seem to have sources in common but John seems to stand alone to a great extent. The Gospels of Mark, Matthew and Luke date to about 65 to 85. The Gospel of John was composed around 90 to 95.

Each writer remembered their stories differently and each had their personal take on the faith. Stories were told through memory blurred with time and slanted by what they wished to convey through the tales they told.

The eighth chapter of Luke starts a story about Mary of Magdala.

Now after this [Jesus] made his way through towns and villages preaching, and proclaiming the Good News of the kingdom of God. With him went the Twelve, as well as certain women who had been cured of evil spirits and ailments: Mary surnamed the Magdalene, from whom seven demons had gone out, Joanna the wife of Herod's steward Chuza, Susanna, and several others who provided for them out of their own resources.

Mary Magdalene was one of the women who "provided for" Jesus and the Twelve. The women would have been from upper class families and would have at least some control over the flow of money within their families. This idea may fly in the face of what is normally presented as the typical subservient women, but that idea is more fantasy than fact.

All the women, including Mary Magdalene were cured of something. The expulsion of demons was the "catch phrase" for being healed, since it was assumed demonic influences caused illness. One source says that the idea of Mary being delivered from seven demons was a way of explaining that she was a wayward and promiscuous woman set free of the seven deadly sins. But, at this time there was no thought of seven deadly sins. There were over 600 laws on the Jewish books ready to be broken.

One story of a "wayward" woman involves a Pharisee who had invited Jesus to a meal. When he arrived at the Pharisee's house and took his place at table, a woman came in uninvited (or so we are led to believe.) The woman found out that Jesus was dining with the Pharisee. Her conscience and the wish to escape her past deeds had caught up to her in an emotional storm. As a offering to Jesus the woman had brought with her an alabaster jar of ointment. She collapsed at the feet of Jesus, weeping, her tears falling on his feet. Embarrassed, she wiped them away with her hair and kissed his feet. She then anointed them with her ointment, a refreshing and not inexpensive gift. This would have been a very intimate moment, seeing as how a man would not have seen a woman bare headed with her hair down, except in an intimate setting. It could be taken as almost erotic, if it were not for the open and gut-wrenching repentance.

When the Pharisee saw this, he said to himself, "If this man were a prophet, he would know who this woman is that is touching him and he would know of her reputation."

Jesus refuses to condemn her, knowing that such repentance and weeping comes only from a truly contrite heart. He announces "Your faith has saved you, Go in peace." Of course the Pharisee takes exception to Jesus' assumption that he could forgive sins, but that is another story for another book.

Over time the story about the unnamed woman would attach to Mary Magdalene as the story of her salvation. The story is a powerful one, full of human drama, and just the kindling preachers and bishops need to start that emotional fire they so desire. Thus it was told again and again by the greatest Christian orators and connected in their monologs to Mary of Magdala. But even a casual reading of this text suggests that the two women, the broken woman of ill repute and Mary Magdalene, have nothing to do with each other.

Matthew adds another layer to the story. In his account of a similar incident he adds further insights.

Jesus was at Bethany in the house of Simon the leper, when a woman came to him with an alabaster jar filled with expensive ointment, and poured it on the head of Jesus, who was sitting at table. When they saw this, the disciples were indignant. They challenged him saying, "Why did you allow this waste? This could have been sold at a high price and the money given to the poor." Jesus set them straight saying, "Why are you getting so upset? Why are you confronting this woman? When she poured this ointment on my body, she did it to prepare me for my burial. I tell you truthfully, this good news will be proclaimed throughout the world, and what she has done will be remembered." Apparently the ointment used in this story was of a strong kind traditionally used to rub on a corpse to keep the scent of death and rotting flesh down as it decays in the tomb. The act is interpreted as a foreshadowing of Jesus' death. In the first story the ointment was more of a type used to perfume.

Where the first story stresses an openness and vulnerability of the giver and the communion between the giver and receiver of the gift, this one stresses the expense of the gift.

These two stories could be the same, growing and changing out of a single oral tradition of a story told around the fire. In Luke's rendition the Pharisee's name is Simon. In Matthew's story we find Simon the leper. In the last story the anointing is tied more directly to his soon-coming death.

Jesus has already predicted his own death but the apostles had rejected the prophecy and said, "far be it from you" or in our terms, "Come on now. Don't be such a pessimist." These women, who anointed Jesus are the intuitive link to the proper response to the previously rejected prophecy.

At the crucifixion of Jesus there were Mary, Mary, Mary, and John. Mary Magdalene is also named as one of the people at the burial of Jesus. This may explain why it was easy to confuse the unnamed woman with her.

The story, as it is told by Matthew and Mark occurred at Bethany. John bear witness in his Gospel. But this is the home of another Mary. She is Mary, the sister of Martha and Lazarus.

Six days before the Passover, Jesus went to Bethany to visit Lazarus, a friend whom he had raised from the dead. Martha waited on them as he and Lazarus talked. Mary, whom Martha was resentful of for not helping in the kitchen, brought a pound of very costly pure ointment called nard, and with it anointed the feet of Jesus. She then cleaned his feet with her hair.

Judas, who was responsible for the money of the group, but who was using it for his own purpose, objects to the waste and says the money it took to buy such a thing could have fed the poor. Jesus scolds Judas saying, "Leave her alone; she had to keep this for the day of my burial, You have the poor with you always, you will not always have me."

Now we have a combination, at least in part, of the two stories, all three of which point toward the death of Jesus. At the death of Jesus on Golgotha Mary Magdalene is expressly identified along with two other Marys, as one of the women who refused to leave him. All four Gospel, as well as the apocryphal Gospel of Peter say she was present at the tomb. In John she is the first witness to the resurrection of Jesus.

Unlike the men who scattered and ran, who lost faith, who betrayed Jesus, the women stayed. The Gospel of John states:

John 20
New International Version (NIV)
The Empty Tomb

20 *Early on the first day of the week, while it was still dark, Mary Magdalene went to the tomb and saw that the stone had been removed from the entrance. 2 So she came running to Simon Peter and the other disciple, the one Jesus loved, and said, "They have taken the Lord out of the tomb, and we don't know where they have put him!"*

3 So Peter and the other disciple started for the tomb. 4 Both were running, but the other disciple outran Peter and reached the tomb first. 5 He bent over and looked in at the strips of linen lying there but did not go in. 6 Then Simon Peter came along behind him and went straight into the tomb. He saw the strips of linen lying there, 7 as well as the cloth that had been wrapped around Jesus' head. The cloth was still lying in its place, separate from the linen. 8 Finally the other disciple, who had reached the tomb first, also went inside. He saw and believed. 9 (They still did not understand from Scripture that Jesus had to rise from the dead.) 10 Then the disciples went back to where they were staying.

11 Now Mary stood outside the tomb crying. As she wept, she bent over to look into the tomb 12 and saw two angels in white, seated where Jesus' body had been, one at the head and the other at the foot. 13 They asked her, "Woman, why are you crying?"

"They have taken my Lord away," she said, "and I don't know where they have put him." 14 At this, she turned around and saw Jesus standing there, but she did not realize that it was Jesus.

15 He asked her, "Woman, why are you crying? Who is it you are looking for?"

Thinking he was the gardener, she said, "Sir, if you have carried him away, tell me where you have put him, and I will get him."

16 Jesus said to her, "Mary."

She turned toward him and cried out in Aramaic, "Rabboni!" (which means "Teacher").

17 Jesus said, "Do not hold on to me, for I have not yet ascended to the Father. Go instead to my brothers and tell them, 'I am ascending to my Father and your Father, to my God and your God.'"

18 Mary Magdalene went to the disciples with the news: "I have seen the Lord!" And she told them that he had said these things to her.

So, without the printing press, with high rates of illiteracy, and a limitation of the written word, these stories were told and retold, each narrator making his own adjustments, decade upon decade of retelling until the stories began to change and merge and the many Marys became confused.

In the Gnostic traditions many texts were written between 200 and 400 AD and tend to mix and match stories of Mary, the mother of Jesus and Mary of Magdala, his consort. We shall see a bit of this when we briefly examine some Gnostic legends regarding Mary.

These stories of Mary endured because they struck such a deep and enduring chord. She was a whore, a devoted companion, a person freed from the guilt and sadness of her past. She is spiritual and erotic. She is us. Christians may worship the Blessed Virgin, but it is Magdalene with whom they identify.

Women, Mary, and the Church

Jesus himself in his teaching and in his circle empowered women and made them equals to men. This is still reflected in the letters of Paul, who many would view as a misogynist. In the letters of St. Paul (c. 50-60), women are named as full partners, preachers, and deacons in the Christian movement. The Gospel accounts give evidence of Jesus' own attitudes and highlight women whose courage and fidelity stand in marked contrast to the lack of attributes of the men in his company who fled or betrayed him.

However, soon after the faith began to morph into a religion the teaching of Jesus and his rejection of male dominance was being eroded.

The Gospels themselves, were being re-interpreted to suggest emphasis on the authority of "the Twelve," who are all males. The all-male composition of "the Twelve" is expressly used by the Vatican today to exclude women from ordination.

Not surprisingly the figure who most embodies the conflict over the place of women in the "church" is Mary Magdalene.

What They Didn't Like, They Changed

Women in the New Testament are usually glossed over. They had stations and positions; some ran churches out of their home; some were tireless workers; others were prophets. However, when the church fathers sat down to translate the New Testament, they did so in a way that diminished the strengths of the women.

Here is a typical example:

Romans 16 (KJV)
1) I commend unto you Phoebe our sister, which is a servant of the church which is at Cenchrea:
2) That ye receive her in the Lord, as becometh saints, and that ye assist her in whatsoever business she hath need of you: for she hath been a succourer of many, and of myself also.

The word translated here as "servant" is rendered as the word "deacon" for men in that position. Here, Phoebe is a servant. Being a woman who was running a church, Phoebe has always been a controversial figure. Paul calls Phoebe a prostatis (translated "succourer,"). The Greek noun used of Phoebe, prostatis, means a "one standing before, a champion, leader, chief, or a protector." She stood before the people and she stood before God as being responsible for teaching and guiding those under her, both male and female.

In 1 Timothy 3:12, we read the following about Phoebe, in our English Bibles: "I commend unto you Phoebe our sister, minister [or deacon] of the church which is at Cenchrea; . . . for she hath been a ruler of many and of myself also." This is the noun form corresponding to the verb prostatis, translated "rule".

Let us look at the verses in context using the Amplified Bible, which attempts to clarify word meaning. Note all of the female names in the chapter.

Romans 16 (Amplified Bible)
1) Now, I introduce and commend to you our sister Phoebe, a deaconess of the church at Cenchreae,
2) That you may receive her in the Lord [with a Christian welcome], as saints (God's people) ought to receive one another. And help her in whatever matter she may require assistance from you, for she has been a helper of many including myself [shielding us from suffering].
3) Give my greetings to Prisca and Aquila, my fellow workers in Christ Jesus,

4) *Who risked their lives [endangering their very necks] for my life. To them not only I, but also all the churches among the Gentiles give thanks.*

5) *[Remember me] also to the church [that meets] in their house. Greet my beloved Epaenetus, who was a first fruit (first convert) to Christ in Asia.*

6) *Greet Mary, who has worked so hard among you.*

7) *Remember me to Andronicus and Junias, my tribal kinsmen and once my fellow prisoners. They are men held in high esteem among the apostles, who also were in Christ before I was.*

8) *Remember me to Ampliatus, my beloved in the Lord.*

9) *Salute Urbanus, our fellow worker in Christ, and my dear Stachys.*

10) *Greet Apelles, that one tried and ap-proved in Christ (the Messiah). Remember me to those who belong to the household of Aristobulus.*

11) *Greet my tribal kinsman, Herodion, and those in the Lord who belong to the household of Narcissus.*

12) *Salute those workers in the Lord, Tryphaena and Tryphosa. Greet my dear Persis, who has worked so hard in the Lord.*

13) *Remember me to Rufus, eminent in the Lord, also to his mother [who has been] a mother to me as well.*

14) *Greet Asyncritus, Phlegon, Hermes, Patrobas, Hermas, and the brethren who are with them.*

15) Greet Philologus, Julia, Nereus, and his sister, and Olympas, and all the saints who are with them.

16) Greet one another with a holy (conse-crated) kiss. All the churches of Christ (the Messiah) wish to be remembered to you.

17) I appeal to you, brethren, to be on your guard concerning those who create dissensions and difficulties and cause divisions, in opposition to the doctrine (the teaching) which you have been taught. [I warn you to turn aside from them, to] avoid them.

18) For such persons do not serve our Lord Christ, but their own appetites and base desires, and by ingratiating and flattering speech, they beguile the hearts of the unsuspecting and simpleminded [people].

19) For while your loyalty and obedience is known to all, so that I rejoice over you, I would have you well versed and wise as to what is good and innocent and guileless as to what is evil.

20) And the God of peace will soon crush Sa-tan under your feet. The grace of our Lord Jesus Christ (the Messiah) be with you.

21) Timothy, my fellow worker, wishes to be remembered to you, as do Lucius and Jason and Sosipater, my tribal kinsmen.

22) I, Tertius, the writer of this letter, greet you in the Lord.

23) Gaius, who is host to me and to the whole church here, greets you. So do Erastus, the city treasurer, and our brother Quartus.

24) The grace of our Lord Jesus Christ (the Messiah) be with you all. Amen (so be it).

25) Now to Him Who is able to strengthen you in the faith which is in accordance with my Gospel and the preaching of (concerning) Jesus Christ (the Messiah), according to the revelation (the unveiling) of the mystery of the plan of redemption which was kept in silence and secret for long ages,

26) But is now disclosed and through the prophetic Scriptures is made known to all nations, according to the command of the eternal God, [to win them] to obedience to the faith,

27) To [the] only wise God be glory forever-more through Jesus Christ (the Anointed One)! Amen (so be it).

Within the above text there are certain things that stand out. The first is the true rendering of the word "deaconess" in regard to Phoebe. The second is the positional listing of certain names. Prisca, also known as Priscilla, and Aquila, for example, shows that the woman, Prisca was likely in the position of authority in the writer's mind.

In I Timothy 3: 4, 5, 12; and 5:17, Paul tells men to "rule well" their own households. These men are told to "rule" their households, as Paul tells us that Phoebe "ruled" him and many others. Phoebe held the same relation to the church at Cenchrea, that Paul says church officials should hold to their own children and household. We can see that the men should take good care of them, not "rule" them. These passages have no direct reference to rule, or government. In Titus 3:8, 14, the word is translated "maintain." This is a better rendering of the word.

Now the Apostle Paul makes use of the verb form of this word in I Timothy 5:14 (KJV), "I will that the younger women marry, bear children, guide the house (oikodespotein), give none occasion to the adversary to speak reproachfully."

The Revised Version does the word a bit more justice and translates it, "rule the household." Is Paul saying the women are the authority of the home? In these times, the women were expected to run the household. Men did not have much to do with the daily decisions of household, children, or even the domestic help, such as slaves.

In Titus 2, Paul instructs the elder women to teach the young women to be "keepers at home". The Greek word translated "keepers at home" (KJV) or "homemakers" (NKJV) is oikouros. This compound word is from oikos- house, household, family; and a guard, guardian, a watcher, a warden. We think of a warden as a masculine position of authority.

It seems that our beliefs are colored by our society. One must attempt to take away the veil of looking at the 1611 society in which the King James' Version translators were immersed to find the truth. After the Geneva Bible and the King James' Bible were accepted as "The Word of God", other Bibles translations were expected to follow their meaning closely. Thus, many modern translators may see the truth more clearly than they can convey to the masses. Error propagates error, and the errors compound in time.

As a footnote, it is interesting to see that is Acts 18, Priscilla instructs Apollos, the man who some think wrote the book of Hebrews. It is also possible that Priscilla contributed to the book of Hebrews, but these things are never clearly mentioned in the Bible and cannot be proven until further evidence is uncovered.

At times, those translating the Bible simply chose to do away with a woman by changing their name to that of a man.

In Romans 16:7, Paul praises a woman named Junia as "outstanding among the apostles."

KJV Romans 16:7 - "Salute Andronicus and Junia, my kinsmen, and my fellow-prisoners, who are of note among the apostles, who also were in Christ before me."

Note in the King James' Version the name, Junia, is a feminine name, but she is referred to as "kinsmen". Now, look at some other translations.

Young's Literal Translation (YLT)
Romans 16:7 - "salute Andronicus and Junias, my kindred, and my fellow-captives, who are of note among the apostles, who also have been in Christ before me."

New International Reader's Version (NIRV)
Romans 16:7 - Greet Andronicus and Junias, my relatives. They have been in prison with me. They are leaders among the apostles. They became believers in Christ before I did.

Bibles and commentators generally utilize Greek New Testaments in their translation and interpretive pursuit. The Greek source documents are given names and the copies are tracked like a family tree. Both the source documents UBS4 and NA27 Greek New Testaments show Iounian accented with a circumflex accent over the alpha, which indicates "Junias" as being a contracted form of Junianus, a male name. Support for "Junias" is attested to by B2 , D2, and a number of minuscules dated from the 9th to 14th century.

No one translating or commenting on this verse prior to the 13th century questioned that this apostle was a woman. Before that time, most translations and copies agreed that Junia was a female who was called an apostle by Paul.

St. John Chrysostom wrote of Romans 16:7, "O how great is the devotion of this woman that she should be counted worthy of the appellation of apostle!"

Some time between the 9th and 13th century, as the church continued to oppress and diminish women, the idea of a female apostle became less tolerable and the verse was altered to fit the prevailing views of the time, an act that was done far more frequently than we would think.

Translators made up the name "Junias" to substitute for the actual name. However, the name that seemed to be the masculine form of the name they were attempting to eradicate was not a real name. No other person in any text has the name, Junias. This was an act she did not deserve. She was suffering along side the men in prison and was being tortured for the sake of the Gospel.

Early Christians under the oppression of Rome had to suffer to proclaim Jesus Christ as Lord. Junia and Andronicus, (perhaps her husband), were called apostles because they had suffered and were imprisoned.

According to Romans 16:7, Junia had become a convert of Jesus before Paul. Since Paul was converted just a few years after the Resurrection of Christ, Junia must have been one of the earliest converts to Christianity and could have been one of the founders of the church at Rome.

There was a sea-change or change of opinion in society between the times of the Old and New Testaments. The place of women in New Testament society was limited. Jesus, being often found in the company of women, was looked at as odd and skating on the raw edge of what was permissible in society at the time. As we have read the stories of women in positions of authority, you will notice that most of them (not all, but most) come from the Old Testament. The place of women in society was becoming more and more limited. Their defined place in the Christian world would become subservient and meaningless. If a woman were to attempt to assert herself, it resulted in social upheaval and her being punished or becoming an outcast.

Although the idea of women being pastors fell into the social trap, which seems so often to ensnare the truth, it is very obvious in the early days of the church, women were not only included, but were some of the first pastors. John's greeting in his second letter did not address the church as the elect or chosen lady, as some would have us believe, but instead the greeting was to a specific woman, who was shepherding a church. Yes, she was a pastor. What's more, the letter is so personal that it was addressed to her, not by the general salutation of "chosen by God", but by her name, which means "chosen by God." My name is Joseph, which means, "he shall add." Her name was Kyria, which is a feminine form of, "one who is chosen or elected by God." When rendered into an English version the name is "Electa."

Kyria, or Electra, has been swept under the rug where the church sweeps ideas they wish would go quietly into the night. Women in the priesthood? John had no problem with it.

Let's look at the modern NIV translation and then compare it to two older, more literal translations.

2 John 1
New International Version (NIV)

1) *The elder,*

To the lady chosen by God and to her children, whom I love in the truth – and not I only, but also all who know the truth –

2) because of the truth, which lives in us and will be with us forever:

2 John 1

Young's Literal Translation (YLT)

1) The Elder to the choice Kyria, and to her children, whom I love in truth, and not I only, but also all those having known the truth,

2)because of the truth that is remaining in us, and with us shall be to the age,

2 John 1:5

and now I beseech thee, Kyria, not as writing to thee a new command, but which we had from the beginning, that we may love one another, (YLT)

2 John 1

Wycliffe New Testament (WYC)

1) The elder man, to the chosen lady [The elder man to the lady Electa], and to her children, which I love in truth; and not I alone, but also all men that know truth [but and all men that knew truth]...

I ask you, who are we to argue with the apostle, John?

Jesus' opinion and placement of women in his ministry flew in the face of the established male dominated role in religion. Jews had gone from a time when women such as Deborah were leaders and judges (See Judges chapters 4 and 5) to a time where only men could be religious figures. Jesus saw women as equals.

Although Jesus rejected male dominance, as symbolized in his commissioning of Mary Magdalene to spread word of the Resurrection, male dominance gradually made a powerful comeback within the Jesus movement. But for that to happen, the commissioning of Mary Magdalene had to be reinvented. One sees that very thing under way in the Gospel of Mary.

For example, Peter's preeminence is elsewhere taken for granted (in Matthew, Jesus says, "You are Peter and on this rock I will build my Church"). Here, he defers to her:

Peter said to Mary, "Sister, we know that the Savior loved you more than all other women. Tell us the words of the Savior that you remember, the things which you know that we don't because we haven't heard them."

Mary responded, "I will teach you about what is hidden from you." And she began to speak these words to them.

Mary recalls her vision, a kind of esoteric description of the ascent of the soul. The disciples Peter and Andrew are disturbed—not by what she says, but by how she knows it. And now a jealous Peter complains to his fellows, "Did [Jesus] choose her over us?" This draws a sharp rebuke from another apostle, Levi, who says, "If the Savior made her worthy, who are you then for your part to reject her?"

That was the question not only about Mary Magdalene, but about women generally. It should be no surprise, given how successfully the excluding dominance of males established itself in the church of the "Fathers," that the Gospel of Mary was one of the texts shunted aside in the fourth century. As that text shows, the early image of this Mary as a trusted apostle of Jesus, reflected even in the canonical Gospel texts, proved to be a major obstacle to establishing that male dominance, which is why, whatever other "heretical" problems this gospel posed, that image had to be recast as one of subservience.

Simultaneously, the emphasis on sexuality as the root of all evil served to subordinate all women. The ancient Roman world was rife with flesh-hating spiritualities—Stoicism, Manichaeism, Neoplatonism—and they influenced Christian thinking just as it was jelling into "doctrine." Thus the need to disempower the figure of Mary Magdalene, so that her succeeding sisters in the church would not compete with men for power, meshed with the impulse to discredit women generally. This was most efficiently done by reducing them to their sexuality, even as sexuality itself was reduced to the realm of temptation, the source of human unworthiness. All of this— from the sexualizing of Mary Magdalene, to the emphatic veneration of the virginity of Mary, the mother of Jesus, to the embrace of celibacy as a clerical ideal, to the marginalizing of female devotion, to the recasting of piety as self-denial, particularly through penitential cults—came to a kind of defining climax at the end of the sixth century. It was then that all the philosophical, theological and ecclesiastical impulses curved back to Scripture, seeking an ultimate imprimatur for what by then was a firm cultural prejudice. It was then that the rails along which the church—and the Western imagination— would run were set.

Pope Gregory I (c. 540-604) was born an aristocrat and served as the prefect of the city of Rome. After his father's death, he gave everything away and turned his palatial Roman home into a monastery, where he became a lowly monk. It was a time of plague, and indeed the previous pope, Pelagius II, had died of it. When the saintly Gregory was elected to succeed him, he at once emphasized penitential forms of worship as a way of warding off the disease. His pontificate marked a solidifying of discipline and thought, a time of reform and invention both. But it all occurred against the backdrop of the plague, a doom-laden circumstance in which the abjectly repentant Mary Magdalene, warding off the spiritual plague of damnation, could come into her own. With Gregory's help, she did.

Known as Gregory the Great, he remains one of the most influential figures ever to serve as pope, and in a famous series of sermons on Mary Magdalene, given in Rome in about the year 591, he put the seal on what until then had been a common but unsanctioned reading of her story. With that, Mary's conflicted image was, in the words of Susan Haskins, author of Mary Magdalene: Myth and Metaphor, "finally settled...for nearly fourteen hundred years."

It all went back to those Gospel texts. Cutting through the exegetes' careful distinctions—the various Marys, the sinful women — that had made the combining of the figures difficult to sustain, Gregory, standing on his own authority, offered his decoding of the relevant Gospel texts. He established the context within which their meaning was measured from then on:

She whom Luke calls the sinful woman, whom John calls Mary, we believe to be the Mary from whom seven devils were ejected according to Mark. And what did these seven devils signify, if not all the vices?

There it was — the woman of the "alabaster jar" named by the pope himself as Mary of Magdala. He defined her:

It is clear, brothers, that the woman previously used the unguent to perfume her flesh in forbidden acts. What she therefore displayed more scandalously, she was now offering to God in a more praiseworthy manner. She had coveted with earthly eyes, but now through penitence these are consumed with tears. She displayed her hair to set off her face, but now her hair dries her tears. She had spoken proud things with her mouth, but in kissing the Lord's feet, she now planted her mouth on the Redeemer's feet. For every delight, therefore, she had had in herself, she now immolated herself. She turned the mass of her crimes to virtues, in order to serve God entirely in penance.

The address "brothers" is the clue. Through the Middle Ages and the Counter-Reformation, into the modern period and against the Enlightenment, monks and priests would read Gregory's words, and through them they would read the Gospels' texts themselves. Chivalrous knights, nuns establishing houses for unwed mothers, courtly lovers, desperate sinners, frustrated celibates and an endless succession of preachers would treat Gregory's reading as literally the gospel truth. Holy Writ, having recast what had actually taken place in the lifetime of Jesus, was itself recast.

The men of the church who benefited from the recasting, forever spared the presence of females in their sanctuaries, would not know that this was what had happened. Having created a myth, they would not remember that it was mythical. Their Mary Magdalene—no fiction, no composite, no betrayal of a once venerated woman—became the only Mary Magdalene that had ever existed.

This obliteration of the textual distinctions served to evoke an ideal of virtue that drew its heat from being a celibate's vision, conjured for celibates. Gregory the Great's overly particular interest in the fallen woman's past—what that oil had been used for, how that hair had been displayed, that mouth—brought into the center of church piety a vaguely prurient energy that would thrive under the licensing sponsorship of one of the church's most revered reforming popes. Eventually, Magdalene, as a denuded object of Renaissance and Baroque painterly preoccupation, became a figure of nothing less than holy pornography, guaranteeing the ever-lustful harlot—if lustful now for the ecstasy of holiness—a permanent place in the Catholic imagination.

Thus Mary of Magdala, who began as a powerful woman at Jesus' side, "became," in Haskins' summary, "the redeemed whore and Christianity's model of repentance, a manageable, controllable figure, and effective weapon and instrument of propaganda against her own sex." There were reasons of narrative form for which this happened. There was a harnessing of sexual restlessness to this image. There was the humane appeal of a story that emphasized the possibility of forgiveness and redemption. But what most drove the anti-sexual sexualizing of Mary Magdalene was the male need to dominate women. In the Catholic Church, as elsewhere, that need is still being met.

This ends excerpts and quotes from the Smithsonian article.

Luke does not name her as the women who washes the feet of Jesus with her hair.

Luke 7 (King James version)

36 And one of the Pharisees desired him that he would eat with him. And he went into the Pharisee's house, and sat down to meat.

37 And, behold, a woman in the city, which was a sinner, when she knew that Jesus sat at meat in the Pharisee's house, brought an alabaster box of ointment,

38 And stood at his feet behind him weeping, and began to wash his feet with tears, and did wipe them with the hairs of her head, and kissed his feet, and anointed them with the ointment.

39 Now when the Pharisee which had bidden him saw it, he spake within himself, saying, This man, if he were a prophet, would have known who and what manner of woman this is that toucheth him: for she is a sinner.

40 And Jesus answering said unto him, Simon, I have somewhat to say unto thee. And he saith, Master, say on.

41 There was a certain creditor which had two debtors: the one owed five hundred pence, and the other fifty.

42 And when they had nothing to pay, he frankly forgave them both. Tell me therefore, which of them will love him most?

43 Simon answered and said, I suppose that he, to whom he forgave most. And he said unto him, Thou hast rightly judged.

44 And he turned to the woman, and said unto Simon, Seest thou this woman? I entered into thine house, thou gavest me no water for my feet: but she hath washed my feet with tears, and wiped them with the hairs of her head.

45 Thou gavest me no kiss: but this woman since the time I came in hath not ceased to kiss my feet.

46 My head with oil thou didst not anoint: but this woman hath anointed my feet with ointment.

47 Wherefore I say unto thee, Her sins, which are many, are forgiven; for she loved much: but to whom little is forgiven, the same loveth little.

48 And he said unto her, Thy sins are forgiven.

49 And they that sat at meat with him began to say within themselves, Who is this that forgiveth sins also?

50 And he said to the woman, Thy faith hath saved thee; go in peace.

There is never a name given to the woman caught in the act of adultery.

John 8 (King James Version)

1 Jesus went unto the mount of Olives.

2 And early in the morning he came again into the temple, and all the people came unto him; and he sat down, and taught them.

3 And the scribes and Pharisees brought unto him a woman taken in adultery; and when they had set her in the midst,

4 They say unto him, Master, this woman was taken in adultery, in the very act.

5 Now Moses in the law commanded us, that such should be stoned: but what sayest thou?

6 This they said, tempting him, that they might have to accuse him. But Jesus stooped down, and with his finger wrote on the ground, as though he heard them not.

7 So when they continued asking him, he lifted up himself, and said unto them, He that is without sin among you, let him first cast a stone at her.

8 And again he stooped down, and wrote on the ground.

9 And they which heard it, being convicted by their own conscience, went out one by one, beginning at the eldest, even unto the last: and Jesus was left alone, and the woman standing in the midst.

10 When Jesus had lifted up himself, and saw none but the woman, he said unto her, Woman, where are those thine accusers? hath no man condemned thee?

11 She said, No man, Lord. And Jesus said unto her, Neither do I condemn thee: go, and sin no more.

12 Then spake Jesus again unto them, saying, I am the light of the world: he that followeth me shall not walk in darkness, but shall have the light of life.

The only clear history we have is a single statement that it was Mary that was once demon-possessed.

Luke 8 (King James Version)

1 And it came to pass afterward, that he went throughout every city and village, preaching and shewing the glad tidings of the kingdom of God: and the twelve were with him,

2 And certain women, which had been healed of evil spirits and infirmities, Mary called Magdalene, out of whom went seven devils,

3 And Joanna the wife of Chuza Herod's steward, and Susanna, and many others, which ministered unto him of their substance.

Here is what we know with certainty:

She was a woman who followed Jesus as he ministered and preached.

Luke 8:1-3: Afterward, Jesus journeyed from one town and village to another, preaching and proclaiming the good news of the kingdom of God. Accompanying him were the Twelve and some women who had been cured of evil spirits and infirmities, Mary, called Magdalene, from whom seven demons had gone out, Joanna, the wife of Herod's steward Chuza, Susanna, and many others who provided for them out of their resources.

She was there when Jesus was crucified.

Mark 15:40: There were also some women looking on from a distance, among whom were Mary Magdalene, and Mary the mother of James the Less and Joses, and Salome.

Matthew 27:56: Among them was Mary Magdalene, and Mary the mother of James and Joseph, and the mother of the sons of Zebedee.

John 19:25: But standing by the cross of Jesus were His mother, and His mother's sister, Mary the wife of Clopas, and Mary Magdalene.

She continued to believe in Jesus after he was killed.

Mark 15:47: Mary Magdalene and Mary the mother of Joses were looking on to see where He was laid.

Matthew 27:61: And Mary Magdalene was there, and the other Mary, sitting opposite the grave.

Matthew 28:1: Now after the Sabbath, as it began to dawn toward the first day of the week, Mary Magdalene and the other Mary came to look at the grave.

Mark 16:1: When the Sabbath was over, Mary Magdalene, and Mary the mother of James, and Salome, bought spices, so that they might come and anoint Him.

She was the first to realize and announce the resurrection of Jesus.

John 20:1: Now on the first day of the week Mary Magdalene came early to the tomb, while it was still dark, and saw the stone already taken away from the tomb.

Mark 16:9: Now after He had risen early on the first day of the week, He first appeared to Mary Magdalene, from whom He had cast out seven demons.

John 20:18: Mary Magdalene came, announcing to the disciples, "I have seen the Lord," and that He had said these things to her.

Luke 24: But at daybreak on the first day of the week [the women] took the spices they had prepared and went to the tomb. They found the stone rolled away from the tomb; but when they entered, they did not find the body of the Lord Jesus. While they were puzzling over this, behold, two men in dazzling garments appeared to them. They were terrified and bowed their faces to the ground. They said to them, "Why do you seek the living one among the dead?

He is not here, but he has been raised. Remember what he said to you while he was still in Galilee, that the Son of Man must be handed over to sinners and be crucified, and rise on the third day." And they remembered his words.

Then they returned from the tomb and announced all these things to the eleven and to all the others.

The women were Mary Magdalene, Joanna, and Mary the mother of James; the others who accompanied them also told this to the apostles, but their story seemed like nonsense and they did not believe them.

Beyond the Bible we have little information on Mary. There are other books wherein she is mentioned and one book which was purported to be written by her. From what we know so far we can conclude the she is hopeful and strong. She is dedicated and educated. She could have come from an upwardly mobile family, which owned fishing boats. She was unconcerned with the limitations society wished to place upon her. Her love and devotion overcame her fear of gossip or ridicule.

There are myths and legends surrounding Mary.

Some of her personality is captured in a Gospel bearing her name. The reader is strongly cautioned regarding the validity of this gospel. The Gospel of Mary is presumed written long after the death of Mary and is likely a forgery. However, on the off chance it was told to someone by Mary and written down later I present it here along with the Gospel of Philip, which seems to confirm the general content of the Gospel of Mary. These two gospels are found in the back of this book.

In "Pistis Sophia," a Gnostic text written between 200 and 300 AD Jesus speaks to Mary saying:

Mary, you are blessed and I shall complete you with all mysteries on high. Speak openly (freely) for I know your heart is set on heaven more than all your brothers."

The book goes on to say "Mary became a pure spirit."

All through Gnostic literature the equality of women is stressed. The placement of Mary Magdalene is stated and re-stated as that of the primary apostle. She was the one who was closest to Jesus. It was to Mary he confided the hidden mysteries of the Kingdom. Mary had the deeper understanding of his teachings. It was to Mary he said, "speak openly and freely for I know your heart desires the Kingdom of Heaven more than any of your brothers." Mary supported him. Mary followed him. Mary did not run away when the Romans were breathing down their necks. Mary was the one he appeared to after he was placed in his tomb, and it was Mary who, according to the Gnostic writings, was his intimate consort and had the complete picture of the mysteries of heaven as they were passed to her directly from the mouth of Jesus.

None of this set well with the male apostles or the Pharisees, who were watching the power structure they had built and secured threatened.

History is written, canon is chosen, and scriptures are altered by the victors. In the race between the various branches of Christianity the one that won now calls the others heretics. The Gnostic were suppressed and their scriptures burned. All traces of Gnostic thought and doctrine was removed. Then came the great Gnostic Cathar genocide by the Catholic church in the 1200's. Not a Gnostic was to be left alive. Even the Gospel of John was reconsidered for canon because it smacked of Gnostic influence. Only now have we begun to rediscover the various roots and branches that were alive and well on the Christian family tree. In Gnostic Christianity women were leaders and people needed no priests or popes to reach heaven for them. The kingdom was found within each of us. As it is now. No wonder the church sought to destroy this doctrine to save their thrones.

Gnostic and Other Legends

This chapter contains information derived from sources that are considered less than reliable. The information is gathered from Gnostic sources, apocryphal literature, and oral traditions.

Mary Magdalene was of the district of Magdala, on the shores of the Sea of Galilee, where stood her families castle, called Magdalon; she was the sister of Lazarus and of Martha, and they were the children of parents reputed noble, or, as some say, royal descendants of the House of David. On the death of their father, Syrus, they inherited vast riches and possessions in land, which were equally divided between them.

Her discreet sister, Martha, frequently rebuked her for these disorders and at length persuaded her to listen to the exhortations of Jesus, through which her heart was touched and converted. The seven demons which possessed her, and which were expelled by Jesus, were the seven deadly sins common to us all. The struggles of these seven principal faults are; first, Gluttony or the pleasures of the palate; secondly, Fornication; thirdly, Covetousness, which means Avarice, or, the love of money, fourthly, Anger; fifthly, Dejection; sixthly,

"Accidie," which is the sin of spiritual sloth or sluggishness; and seventhly, kenodocila which means ego, foolish pride or vain glory. On one occasion Martha entertained the Savior in her house, and, being anxious to feast him worthily, she was 'cumbered with much serving.' Mary, meanwhile, sat at the feet of Jesus, and heard his words, which completed the good work of her conversion; and when, some time afterwards, he supped in the house of Simon the Pharisee, she followed him thither and she brought an alabaster box of ointment and began to wash his feet with tears, and did wipe them with the hair of her head, and kissed his feet, and anointed them with ointment - and He said unto her, Thy sins are forgiven.'

Tradition relates that afterwards in Italy, Mary Magdalene visited the Emperor Tiberias (14-37 AD) and proclaimed to him about Christ's Resurrection. According to tradition, she took him an egg as a symbol of the Resurrection, a symbol of new life with the words: "Christ is Risen!" Then she told Tiberias that, in his Province of Judea, Jesus the Nazarene, a holy man, a maker of miracles, powerful before God and all mankind, was executed on the instigation of the Jewish High-Priests and the sentence affirmed by the procurator Pontius Pilate. Tiberias responded that no one could rise from the dead, anymore than the egg she held could turn red. Miraculously, the egg immediately began to turn red as testimony to her words.

Then, and by her urging, Tiberias had Pilate removed from Jerusalem to Gaul, where he later suffered a horrible sickness and an agonizing death.

Suggestions of commentators and legend continues her story. Fourteen years after the ascension, Lazarus with his two sisters, Martha and Mary; with Maximin, one of the seventy-two disciples, from whom they had received baptism; Cedon, the blind man whom our Savior had restored to sight; and Marcella, the handmaiden who attended on the two sisters, were by the Jews set adrift in a vessel without sails, oars, or rudder; but, guided by Providence, they were safely borne over the sea till they landed in a certain harbor which proved to be Marseilles, in the country now called France.

The people of the land were pagans, and refused to give the holy pilgrims food or shelter; so they were fain to take refuge under the porch of a temple and Mary Magdalene preached to the people, reproaching them for their senseless worship of idols; and though at first they would not listen, yet being after a time convinced by her eloquence, and by the miracles performed by her and by her sister, they were converted and baptized. And Lazarus became, after the death of the good Maximin, the first bishop of Marseilles.

These things being accomplished, Mary Magdalene retired to the cliffs not far from the city. It was a frightful barren wilderness and in the midst of horrid rocks she lived in the caves of Sainte-Baume; there for thirty years she devoted herself to solitary penance for the sins of her past life, which she had never ceased to bewail bitterly. During this long seclusion, she was never seen or heard of, and it was supposed that she was dead.

Assumption of Mary Magdalene, by José Antolinez

She fasted so rigorously, that but for the occasional visits of the angels, and the comfort bestowed by celestial visions, she might have perished. She was given the Holy Eucharist by angels as her only food. Every day during the last years of her penance, the angels came down from heaven and carried her up in their arms into regions where she was ravished by the sounds of unearthly harmony, and beheld the glory and the joy prepared for the sinner that repenteth.

One day a certain hermit, who dwelt in a cell on one of those wild mountains, having wandered farther than usual from his home, beheld this wondrous vision - the Magdalene in the arms of ascending angels, who were singing songs of triumph as they bore her upwards; and the hermit, when he had a little recovered from his amazement, returned to the city of Marseilles, and reported what he had seen.

Some say she did do die in France but returned to Rome in her old-age. From Rome, Mary Magdalene, moved to Ephesus where she unceasingly labored the holy Apostle John, who with her wrote the first 20 Chapters of his Gospel (John 1-9, John 10-20). There the saint finished her earthly life and was buried. Mary was transported miraculously, just before she died, to the chapel of St. Maximin, where she received the last sacraments. She died when she was 72.

In 899 the Emperor Leo VI transported her alleged relics to a monastery in Constantinople. It was not until the tenth century that devotion to Mary Magdalene, the composite saint, took root in the west.

The Couple

The disciples said to Jesus, "...

... deny. Mary is worthy of it ...

..." Jesus said to them, "My wife ...

... she will be able to be my disciple ...

Gospel of Jesus' Wife

And the companion (Consort) was Mary of Magdala. The Lord loved Mary more than all the other disciples and he kissed her often on her mouth (the text is missing here and the word is assumed). The others saw his love for Mary and asked him: "Why do thou love her more than all of us?" The Savior replied, "Why do I not love you in the same way I love her?"

Gospel of Philip

Peter said to Mary; "Sister we know that the Savior loved you more than all other woman. Tell us the words of the

Savior that you remember and know, but have we heard and do not know.

Mary answered him and said; "I will tell you what He hid from you."

Gospel of Mary Magdalene

114. Simon Peter said to them: Send Mary away from us, for women are not worthy of this life. Jesus said: See, I will draw her into me so that I make her male, in order that she herself will become a living spirit like you males. For every female who becomes male will enter the Kingdom of the Heavens

Gospel of Thomas

The evidence of the gospels, which were not included as canon, has been examined. Related biblical texts have been studied. The testimony of historians of the day has been presented. Accounts and letters of kings and church leaders have been read. We have seen how history was re-written to conform to society and orthodoxy. We have looked inside the little-known worlds of Jesus of Nazareth and Mary of Magdala. Now, it is time to decide which evidence is acceptable and which is not. If it is concluded the church authorities hid the truth then it also may be concluded Jesus had a wife and her name was Mary.

A Jewish man, raised by a loving mother, revered and respected women. He supported family and marriage. He was a preacher and was passionate about the truth. He met a woman who was strong, independent, dedicated and devoted, who loved him, followed him, and believed in his vision. He kissed her, taught her, and shared his deepest secrets with her. He became a rabbi and taught throughout the region. He was killed for his beliefs but she continued on, carrying his teachings to others even after his death. She mourned his passing and never loved another man.

Were Jesus and Mary husband and wife?
It is up to you to decide if this was a love story or not.

The History of The Gospel of Philip

The Gospel of Philip is assumed to be one of the sources of Dan Brown's novel, The Da Vinci Code, about Mary Magdalene, Jesus, and their children. The Gospel is one of Gnostic texts found at Nag Hammadi in Egypt in 1945 and belongs to the same collection of Gnostic documents as the more famous Gospel of Thomas.

It has been suggested that the _Gospel of Philip_ was written in the second century B.C. If so, it may be one of the earliest documents containing themes that would later be used in apocryphal literature.

A single manuscript of the _Gospel of Philip_, written in Coptic, was found in the Nag Hammadi library. The collection was a library of thirteen papyrus texts discovered near the town of Nag Hammadi in 1945 by a peasant boy. The writings in these codices comprised 52 documents, most of which were Gnostic in nature.

The codices were probably hidden by monks from the nearby monastery of St. Pachomius when the official Christian Church banned all Gnostic literature around the year 390 A.D

It is believe the original texts were written in Greek during the first or second centuries A.D. The copies contained in the discovered clay jar were written in Coptic in the third or fourth centuries A.D.

The _Gospel Of Philip_ is a list of sayings focusing on man's redemption and salvation as framed by Gnostic theology.

The _Gospel of Philip_ presented here is based on a comparative study of translations from the Nag Hammadi Codex by Wesley W. Isenberg, Willis Barnstone, The Ecumenical Coptic Project, Bart Ehrman, Marvin Meyer, David Cartlidge, David Dungan, and other sources.

Each verse was weighed against the theological and philosophical beliefs held by the Gnostic community at the time in which the document was penned. All attempts were made to render the most accurate meaning based on the available translations and information.

Exact wording was secondary to the conveyance of the overall meaning as understood by contemporary readers.

When the wording of a verse held two possible meanings or needed expanded definitions, optional translations were placed in parentheses.

The Gospel of Philip

1. A Hebrew makes a Hebrew convert, and they call him a proselyte (novice). A novice does not make another novice. Some are just as they are, and they make others like themselves to receive. It is enough for them that they simply are as they are.

2. The slave seeks only to be set free. He does not hope to attain the estate of his master. The son acts as a son (heir), but the father gives the inheritance to him.

3. Those who inherit the dead are dead, and they inherit the dead. Those who inherit the living are alive. They inherit both the living and the dead. The dead cannot inherit anything. How can the dead inherit anything? When the dead inherits the (singular) living, he shall not die but the dead shall live instead.

4. The Gentile (unbeliever) who does not believe does not die, because he has never been alive, so he could not die. He who has trusted the Truth has found life and is in danger of dying, because he is now alive.

5. Since the day that the Christ came. The cosmos was created, the cities are built (adorned), and the dead carried out.

6. In the days when we were Hebrews we were made orphans, having only our Mother. Yet when we believed in the Messiah (became the ones of Christ), the Mother and Father both came to us.

7. Those who sow in the winter reap in the summer. The winter is this world system. The summer is the other age / dispensation (to come). Let us sow in the world (cosmos) so that we will reap in the summer. Because of this, it is right for us not to pray in the winter. What comes from (follows) the winter is the summer. If anyone reaps in the winter he will not harvest but rather pull it up by the roots and will not produce fruit. Not only does it not produce in winter, but on the Sabbath his field shall be bare.

8. The Christ has come to fully ransom some, to save (restore and heal) others, and to be the propitiation for others. Those who were estranged he ransomed. He purchases them for himself. He saves, heals, and restores those who come to him. These he desires to pledge (in marriage). When he became manifest he ordained the soul as he desired (set aside his own life), but even before this, in the time of the world's beginning, he had ordained the soul (he had laid down his own life). At his appointed time, he came to bring the soul he pledged himself to back to himself. It had come to be under the control of robbers and they took it captive. Yet he saved it, and he paid the price for both the good and the evil of the world.

9. Light and dark, life and death, right and left are brothers. It is impossible for one to be separated from the other. They are neither good, nor evil. A life is not alive without death. Death is not death if one were not alive. Therefore each individual shall be returned to his origin from the beginning. Those who go beyond the world will live forever and are in the eternal present.

10. The names that are given to worldly things cause great confusion. They contort our perception from the real to the unreal. He who hears "God" does not think of the real, but rather has false, preconceived ideas. It is the same with "Father", "Son", "Holy Spirit", "Life", "Light", "Resurrection" and "church (the called out ones)", and all other words. They do not think of the real, but rather they call to mind preconceived, false ideas. They learned the reality of human death. They who are in the world system made them think of the false idea. If they had been in eternity, they would not have designated anything as evil, nor would they have placed things within worldly events (time and place). They are destined for eternity.

11. The only name they should never speak into the world is the name the Father gave himself through the Son. This is the Father's name. It exists that he may be exalted over all things. The Son could not become the Father, unless he was given the Father's name. This name exists so that they may have in their thoughts. They should never speak it. Those who do not have it cannot even think it. But the

truth created names in the world for our sake. It would not be possible to learn the truth without names.

12. The Truth alone is the truth. It is a single thing and a multitude of things. The truth teaches us love alone through many and varied paths.

13. Those who ruled (lower gods) desired to deceive man because they knew man was related to the truly good ones. They took the designation of good and they gave it to those who were not good. They did this so that by way of words they might deceive man and bind him to those who are not good. When they receive favor, they are taken from those who are not good and placed among the good. These are they who had recognized themselves. The rulers (lower gods) had desired to take the free person, and enslave him to themselves forever. Rulers of power fight against man. The rulers do not want him to be saved (recognize himself), so that men will become their masters. For if there is man is saved there is saved there will be no need for sacrifice.

14. When sacrifice began, animals were offered up to the ruling powers. They were offered up to them while the sacrificial animals were still alive. But as they offered them up they were killed. But the Christ was offered up dead to God (the High God), and yet he lived.

15. Before the Christ came, there had been no bread in the world. In paradise, the place where Adam was, there had been many plants as food for wild animals, but paradise had no wheat for man to eat. Man had to be nourished like animals. But the Christ, the perfect man, was sent. He brought the bread of heaven, so that man could eat as he should.

16. The rulers (lower gods) thought what they did was by their own will and power, but the Holy Spirit worked through them without their knowledge to do her will.

17. The truth, which exists from the beginning, is sown everywhere, and everyone sees it being sown, but only a few see the harvest.

18. Some say that Mary conceived by the Holy Spirit. They are in error. They do not know what they are saying. How can a female impregnate another female? Mary is the virgin whom no power defiled. She is great among the problem and curse for the Hebrew Apostles and for those in charge. The ruler (lower god) who attempts to defile this virgin, is himself defiled. The Lord was not going to say, "my father in heaven", unless he really had another father. He would simply have said, "my father".

19. The Lord says to the Disciples, "Come into the house of the Father, but do not bring anything in or take anything out from the father's house.

20.   Jesus (Yeshua) is the secret name; Christ (messiah) is the revealed name. The name "Jesus" (Yeshua) does not occur in any other language. His name is called "Jesus" (Yeshua). In Aramaic his name Messiah, but in Greek it is: Christ (Cristos). In every language he is called the anointed one. The fact that he is Savior (Yeshua) could be fully comprehended only by himself, since it is the Nazarene who reveals the secret things.

21.   Christ has within himself all things; man, angel, mystery (sacraments), and the father.

22.   Those who say that the Lord first died and then arose are in error. He would have to first arise before he could die. If he is not first resurrected, he would die, but God lives and cannot die.

23.   No one will hide something highly valuable in something ostentatious (that would draw attention). More often, one places something of great worth within a number of containers worth nothing. This is how it is with the (human) soul. It is a precious thing placed within a lowly body.

24.   Some are fearful that they will arise (from the dead) naked. Therefore they desire to rise in the flesh. They do not understand that those who choose to wear the flesh are naked. Those who choose to strip themselves of the flesh are the ones who are not naked.

25. Flesh and blood will not be able to inherit the kingdom of God. What is this that will not inherit? It is that which is upon each of us (our flesh). But what will inherit the kingdom is that which belongs to Jesus and is of his flesh and blood. Therefore he says: "He who does not eat my flesh and drink my blood, has no life in him." What is his flesh? It is the word. And his blood is the Holy Spirit. He who has received these has food and drink and clothing.

26. I disagree with those who say the flesh will not arise. They are in error. Tell me what will rise so that we may honor you. You say it is the spirit in the flesh and the light contained in the flesh. But you say there is nothing outside of the flesh (material world). It is necessary to arise in this flesh if everything exists within the flesh.

27. In this world those wearing a garment are more valuable than the garment. In the kingdom of the Heavens the garment is more valuable than the one wearing it.

28. By water and fire the entire realm is purified through the revelations by those who reveal them, and by the secrets through those who keep them. Yet, there are things kept secret even within those things revealed. There is water in baptism and there is fire in the oil of anointing.

29. Jesus took them all by surprise. For he did not reveal himself as he originally was, but he revealed himself as they were capable of perceiving him. He revealed himself to all in their own way. To the great, he revealed himself as great. To the small he was small. he revealed himself to the angels as an angel and to mankind he was a man. Some looked at him and saw themselves. But, throughout all of this, he concealed his words from everyone. However when he revealed himself to his Disciples upon the mountain, he appeared glorious. He was not made small. He became great, but he also made the Disciples great so that they would be capable of comprehending his greatness.

30. He said on that day during his thanksgiving (in the Eucharist): "You have combined the perfect light and the holy spirit along with angels and images."

31. Do not hate the Lamb. Without him it is not possible to see the door to the sheepfold. Those who are naked will not come before the King.

32. The Sons of the Heavenly Man are more numerous than those of the earthly man. If the sons of Adam are numerous although they die, think of how many more Sons the Perfect Man has and these do not die. And they are continually born every instant of time.

33. The Father creates a Son, but it is not possible for the Son to create a son because it is impossible for someone who was just born to have a child. The Son has Brothers, not sons.

34. There is order in things. All those who are born in the world are begotten physically. Some are begotten spiritually, fed by the promise of heaven, which is delivered by the perfect Word from the mouth. The perfect Word is conceived through a kiss and thus they are born. There is unction to kiss one another to receive conception from grace to grace.

35. There were three women named Mary who walked with the Lord all the time. They were his mother, his sister and Mary of Magdala, who was his consort (companion). Thus his mother, his sister and companion (consort) were all named Mary.

36. "Father" and "Son" are single names, "Holy Spirit" is a double name and it is everywhere; above and below, secret and revealed. The Holy Spirit's abode is manifest when she is below. When she is above she is hidden.

37. Saints are served by evil powers (lesser gods). The evil spirits are deceived by the Holy Spirit to think they think they are assisting a common man when they are serving Saints. A follower of the Lord once asked him for a thing from this world. He answered him saying;

Ask you Mother, and she will give you something from another realm.

38. The Apostles said to the students: May all of our offering obtain salt! They had called wisdom salt and without it no offering can become acceptable.

39. Wisdom (Sophia) is barren. She has no children but she is called Mother. Other are found (adopted) by the Holy Spirit, and she has many children.

40. That which the Father has belongs to the Son, but he cannot possess it when he is young (small). When he comes of age all his father has will be given to the son.

41. Those who do not follow the path are born of the Spirit, and they stray because of her. By this same spirit (breath / life force), the fire blazes and consumes.

42. Earthly Wisdom is one thing, and death is another. Earthly Wisdom is simply wisdom, but death is the wisdom of death, and death is the one who understands death. Being familiar with death is minor wisdom.

43. There are animals like the bull and donkey that are submissive to man. There are others that live in the wilderness. Man plows the field

with submissive animals, and uses the harvest to feed himself as well as all the animals, domesticated or wild. So it is with the Perfect Man. Through submissive powers he plows and provides a for all things to exist. He causes all things to come together into existence, whether good or evil, right or left.

44 The Holy Spirit is the shepherd; guiding everyone and every power (lower ruler / lesser gods) whether they are submissive, rebellious or feral. She controls them, subdues them, and keeps them bridled, whether they wish it or not.

45. Adam was created beautiful. One would expect his children to be noble. If he were not created but rather born, one would expect his children to be noble. But He was both created and born. Is this nobility?

46. Adultery occurred first and then came murder. And Cain was conceived in adultery because he was the serpent's (Satan's) son. He became a murderer just like his father. He killed his brother. When copulation occurs between those who are not alike, this is adultery.

47. God is a dyer. Just as a good and true dye penetrates deep into fabric to dye it permanently from within (not a surface act), so God has baptized what He dyes into an indelible dye, which is water.

48. It is impossible for anyone to see anything in the real world, unless he has become part of it. It is not like at person in this world. When one looks like the sun he can see it without being part of it. He sees the sky and the earth or any other thing without having to be part of it. So it is with this world, but in the other world you must become what you see (see what you become). To see spirit you must be spirit. To see Christ you must be Christ. To see the father you must be the Father. In this way you will see everything but yourself. If you look at yourself you will become what you see.

49. Faith receives, but love gives. No one can receive without faith. No one can love without giving. Believe and you shall receive. Love and you shall give. If you give without love, you shall receive nothing. Whoever has not received the Lord, continues to be a Jew.

50. The Apostles who came before us called him Jesus, The Nazarene, and The Messiah. Of these names, Jesus (Yeshua), The Nazarene (of the rite of the Nazarites), and The Messiah (Christ), the last name is the Christ, the first is Jesus, and the middle name is The Nazarene. Messiah has two meanings; the anointed one and the measured one. Jesus (Yeshua) means The Atonement (Redemption / Payment). 'Nazara' means Truth. Therefore, the Nazarite is The Truth. The Christ is The Measured One, the Nazarite (Truth) and Jesus (Redemption) have been measured (are the measurement).

51. The pearl which is thrown into the mud is not worth less than it was before. If it is anointed with balsam oil it is valued no higher. It is as valuable as its owner perceives it to be. So it is with the children of God. Whatever becomes of them, they are precious in their Father's eyes.

52. If you say you are a Jew it will not upset anyone.
If you say you are Roman, on no will care. If you claim to be a Greek, foreigner, slave, or a free man no one will be the least bit disturbed. But, if you claim to belong to Christ everyone will take heed (be concerned). I hope to receive this title from him. Those who are worldly would not be able to endure when they hear the name.

53. A god is a cannibal, because men are sacrificed to it. Before men were sacrificed, animals were sacrificed. Those they are sacrificed to are not gods.

54. Vessels of glass and vessels of clay are always made with fire. But if a glass vessel should break it is recast, because it is made in a single breath. If clay vessel breaks it is destroyed, since it came into being without breath.

55. A donkey turning a millstone walked a hundred miles but when it was untied it was in the same place it started. There are those who go on long journeys but do not progress. When evening comes (when the journey ends), they have discovered no city, no village, no

construction site, no creature (natural thing), no power (ruler), and no angel. They labored and toiled for nothing (emptiness).

56. The thanksgiving (Eucharist) is Jesus. For in Aramaic they call him farisatha, which means, "to be spread out. This is because Jesus came to crucify the world.

57. The Lord went into the place where Levi worked as a dyer. He took 72 pigments and threw them into a vat. When he drew out the result it was pure white. He said, "This is how the Son of Man has come. He is a dyer."

58. Wisdom, which they call barren, is the mother of the angels. And the companion (Consort) was Mary of Magdala. The Lord loved Mary more than all the other disciples and he kissed her often on her mouth (the text is missing here and the word is assumed). The others saw his love for Mary asked him: "Why do thou love her more than all of us?" The Savior replied, "Why do I not love you in the same way I love her?" While a blind person and a person who sees are both in the dark, there is no difference, but when the light comes, the one who sees shall behold the light, but he who is blind will remain in darkness.

59. The Lord says: "Blessed is he who existed before you came into being, for he is and was and shall (continue to) be.

60. The supremacy of man is not evident, but it is hidden. Because of this he is master of the animals, which are stronger (larger) than him, in ways both evident and not. This allows the animals to survive. But, when man departs from them, they bite and kill and devour each other because they have no food. Now they have food because man cultivated the land.

61. If one goes down into the water (is baptized) and comes up having received nothing, but claims to belong to Christ, he has borrowed against the name at a high interest rate. But if one receives the Holy Spirit, he has been given the name as a gift. He who has received a gift does not have to pay for it or give it back. If you have borrowed the name you will have to pay it back with interest when it is demanded. This is how the mystery works.

62. Marriage is a sacrament and a mystery. It is grand. For the world is founded upon man, and man founded upon marriage. Consider sex (pure sex), it has great power although its image is defiled.

63. Among the manifestations of unclean spirits there are male and female. The males are those who mate with the souls inhabiting a female form, and the female spirits invite those inhabiting a male form to have sex. Once seized, no one escapes unless they receive both the male and female power that is endued to the Groom with the Bride. The power is seen in the mirrored Bridal-Chamber. When foolish women see a man sitting alone, they want to subdue him,

touch and handle him, and defile him. When foolish men see a beautiful woman sitting alone, they wish to seduce her, draw her in with desire and defile her. But, if the spirits see the man sitting together with his woman, the female spirit cannot intrude upon the man and the male spirit cannot intrude upon the woman. When image and angel are mated, no one can come between the man and woman.

64. He who comes out from the world cannot be stopped. Because he was once in the world he is now beyond both yearning (desire) and fear. He has overcome the flesh and has mastered envy and desire. If he does not leave the world there are forces that will come to seize him, strangle him. How can anyone escape? How can he fear them? Many times men will come and say, "We are faithful, and we hid from unclean and demonic spirits." But if they had been given the Holy Spirit, no unclean spirit would have clung to them. Do not fear the flesh, nor love it. If you fear it, the flesh will become your master. If you love it, the flesh will devour you and render you unable to move.

65. One exists either in this world or in the resurrection or in transition between them. Do not be found in transition. In that world there is both good and evil. The good in it is not good and the evil in it is not evil. There is evil after this world, which is truly evil and it is call the transition. This is what is called death. While we are in this world it is best that we be born into the resurrection, so that we take off the flesh and find rest and not wander within the region of the

transition. Many go astray along the way. Because of this, it is best to go forth from the world before one has sinned.

66. Some neither wish nor are able to act. Others have the will to act but it is best for them if they do not act, because the act they desire to perform would make them a sinner. By not desiring to do a righteous act justice is withheld (not obvious). However, the will always comes before the act.

67. An Apostle saw in a vision people confined to a blazing house, held fast in bonds of fire, crying out as flames came from their breath. There was water in house, and they cried out, "The waters can truly save us. They were misled by their desire. This is called the outermost darkness.

68. Soul and spirit were born of water and fire. From water, fire, and light the children of the Bridal-Chamber are born. The fire is the spirit (anointing), the light is the fire, but not the kind of fire that has form. I speak of the other kind whose form is white and it rains down beauty and splendor.

69. The truth did not come unto the world naked, but it came in types and symbols. The world would not receive it any other way. There is a rebirth together with its symbols. One cannot be reborn through symbols. What can the symbol of resurrection raise, or the Bridal-Chamber with its symbols? One must it is come into the truth through

the imagery. Truth is this Restoration. It is good for those not born to take on the names of the Father, the Son, and the Holy Spirit. They could not have done so on their own. Whoever is not born of them, will have the name (Christ's ones) removed from him. The one who receives them receives the anointing of the spirit and the unction and power of the cross. This is what the Apostles call having the right with the left. When this happens, you no longer belong to Christ, you will be Christ.

70.   The Lord did everything through sacraments (mysteries / symbols): There was Baptism with anointing with thanksgiving (Eucharist) with an Atonement (sacrifice/payment) and Bridal-Chamber.

71. He says: I came to make what is inside the same as the outside and what is below as it is above. I came to bring all of this into one place. He revealed himself through types and symbols. Those who say Christ comes from the place beyond (above) are confused.

72. He who is manifest in heaven is called "one from below." And He who knows the hidden thing is He who is above him. The correct way to say it would be "the inner and the outer or this which is beyond the outer". Because of this, the Lord called destruction "the outer darkness". There is nothing beyond it. He says, "My Father, who is in secret". He says "Go into your inner chamber, shut the door behind you and there pray to your Father who is in secret; He who is

deep within. He is within them all is the Fullness. Beyond Him there is nothing deeper within. The deepest place within is called the uppermost place.

73. Before Christ some came forth. They were not able to go back from where they came. They were no longer able to leave from where they went it. Then Christ came. Those who went in he brought out, and those who went out he brought in.

74. When Eve was still within Adam (man), there had been no death. When she was separated from him, death began. If she were to enter him again and if he were to receive her completely, death would stop.

75. "My God, my God, Oh Lord why did you abandon me?" He spoke these words on the cross. He divided the place and was not there any longer.

76. The Lord arose from the dead. He became as he had been, but his body had been made perfect. He was clothed in true flesh. Our flesh is not true, but rather an image of true flesh, as one beholds in a mirror.

77. The Bridal-Chamber is not for beasts, slaves, or whores. It is for free men and virgins.

78. Through the Holy Spirit we are born again, conceived in Christ, anointed in the spirit, united within us. Only with light can we see ourselves reflected in water or mirror. We are baptized in water and light. It is the light that is the oil of the anointing.

79. There had been three offering vestibules in Jerusalem. One opened to the west called the holy, another opened to the south called the holy of the holy, the third opened to the east called the holy of the holies where the high priest alone was to enter. The Baptism is the holy, the redemption (payment / atonement) is the holy of the holy, and the holy of the holies is the Bridal-Chamber. The Baptism has within it the resurrection and the redemption. Redemption allows entrance into the Bridal-Chamber. The Bridal-Chamber is more exalted than any of these. Nothing compares.

80. Those who pray for Jerusalem love Jerusalem. They are in Jerusalem and they see it now. These are called the holy of the holies.

81. Before the curtain of the Temple was torn we could not see the Bridal-Chamber. All we had was the symbol of the place in heaven. When the curtain was torn from the top to the bottom it made a way for some to ascend.

82. Those who have been clothed in the Perfect Light cannot be seen by the powers, nor can the powers subdue them. Yet one shall be clothed with light in the sacrament (mystery) of sex (being united).

83. If the woman had not been separated from the man, neither would have died. Christ came, to rectify the error of separation that had occurred. He did this by re-uniting them and giving life to those who died. The woman unites with her husband in the bridal-chamber and those who have united in the Bridal-Chamber will not be parted again. Eve separated from Adam because she did not unite with him in the Bridal-Chamber.

84. The soul of man (Adam) was created when breath (spirit) was blown into him. The elements were supplied by his mother. When soul (mind/will) became spirit and were joined together he spoke in word the powers could not understand.

85. Jesus manifested beside the River Jordan with fullness of the kingdom of the Heavens, which existed before the anything. Moreover, he was born as a Son before birth. He was anointed and he anointed. He was atoned and he atoned.

86. If it is right to speak of a mystery. The Father of the all mated with the Virgin who had come down. A fire shone over him on that day. He revealed the power of the Bridal-Chamber. Because of this power his body came into being on that day. He came forth in the Bridal-Chamber in glory because of issued from the Bridegroom to the Bride. This is how Jesus established everything. It was in his

heart. In this same way it is right for each one of the disciples to enter into his rest.

87. Adam came into being from two virgins, from the Spirit and from the virgin earth. Christ was born from a virgin, so that the error which occurred in the beginning would be corrected by him.

88. There were two trees in paradise. One produces beasts, the other produces man. Adam ate from the tree that produced beasts becoming a beast he gave birth to beasts. Because of this, animals were worshipped. God created man and men created gods. This is how the world works; men create gods and they worship their creations. It would have been more appropriate for gods to worship mankind. This would be the way if Adam had eaten from the tree of life, which bore people.

89. The deed of man follow his abilities. These are his strengths and the thing he does with ease. His result is his children who came forth from his times of rest. His work is governed by his work but in his rest he brings forth his sons. This is the sign and symbol, doing works with strength, and producing children in his rest.

90. In this world the slaves are forced to serve the free. In the kingdom of Heaven the free shall serve the slaves and the Bridegroom of the Bridal-Chamber shall serve the guests. Those of the Bridal-Chamber have a single name among them, it is "rest" and they have

no need for any other. The contemplation of the symbol brings enlightenment and great glory. Within those in the Chamber (rest) the glories are fulfilled.

91. Go into the water but do not go down into death, because Christ shall atone for him when he who is baptized comes forth. They were called to be fulfilled in his name. For he said, "We must fulfill all righteousness."

92. Those who say they shall die and then arise are confused. If you do not receive the resurrection while you are alive you will not receive anything when you die. This is why it is said that Baptism is great, because those who receive it shall live.

93. Philip the Apostle said: Joseph the Carpenter planted a grove of trees because he needed wood for his work (craft / trade). He himself made the cross from the trees that he had planted, and his heir hung on that which he had planted. His heir was Jesus, and the tree was the cross. But the tree of life in the midst of the garden (paradise) is the olive tree. From the heart of it comes the anointing through the olive oil and from that comes the resurrection.

94. This world consumes corpses. Everything eaten by (in) the world dies. The truth devours life, but if you eat truth you shall never die. Jesus came (from there) bringing food. And to those wishing it (whom he wished) he gave life, so that they not die.

95. God created the garden (paradise). Man lived in the there, but they did not have God in their hearts and so they gave in to desire. This garden is where it will be said to us, " You may eat this but not eat that, according to your desire." This is the place where I shall choose to eat various things such as being there the tree of knowledge, which slew Adam. In this place the tree of knowledge gave life to man. The Torah is the tree. It has the power to impart the knowledge of good and evil. It did not remove him from the evil or deliver him to good. It simply caused those who had eaten it to die. Death began because truth said, " You can eat this, but do not eat that."

96. The anointing (chrism) is made superior to Baptism, because from the word Chrism we are called Christians (Christ's ones) not because of the word Baptism. And because of Chrism he was called Christ. The Father anointed the Son, and the Son anointed the Apostles, and the Apostles anointed us. He who has been anointed has come to possess all things; he has the resurrection, the light, the cross, and the Holy Spirit. The Father bestowed this upon him in the Bridal-Chamber. The father gave it to the Son who received it freely. The Father was in the Son, and the Son was in the Father. This is the kingdom of Heaven.

97. It was perfectly said by the Lord: Some have attained the kingdom of Heaven laughing. They came forth from the world joyous. Those who belong to Christ who went down into the water immediately came up as lord of everything. He did not laugh because he took

things lightly, but because he saw that everything in this world was worthless compared to the kingdom of Heaven. If he scoffs at the world and sees its worthlessness he will come forth laughing.

98. The Bread and cup, and the oil of anointing (Chrism): There is one superior to them all.

99. The world (system) began in a mistake. He who made this world wished to make it perfect and eternal. He failed (fell away / did not follow through) and did not attain his goal. The world is not eternal, but the children of the world are eternal. They were children and obtained eternity. No one can receive eternity except by becoming a child. The more you are unable to receive, the more you will be unable to give.

100. The cup of the communion (prayer) contains wine and water. It is presented as the symbol of the blood. Over it (because of the blood) we give thanks. It is filled by (with) the Holy Spirit. It (the blood) belongs to the Perfect Man. When we drink we consume the Perfect man

101. The Living Water is a body. It is right that we be clothed with a living body (The Living Man). When he goes down into the water he undresses himself so he may be clothed with the living man.

102. A horse naturally gives birth to a horse, a human naturally gives birth to a human, a god naturally gives birth to a god. The Bridegroom within the Bride give birth to children who are born in the Bridal-

Chamber. The Jews do not spring forth from Greeks (Gentiles), and Christians (those belonging to Christ) do not come from Jews. These who gave birth to Christians were called the chosen generation of the Holy Spirit (living God). The True Man, the Son of Mankind, was the seed that brought forth the sons of Man. This generation is the true ones in the world. This is the place where the children of the Bridal-Chamber dwell.

103. Copulation occurs in this world when man and woman mix (mingle / entwine). Strength joins with weakness. In eternity there is a different kind of mingling that occurs. Metaphorically we call it by the same names, but it is exalted beyond any name we may give it. It transcends brute strength. Where there is no force, there are those who are superior to force. Man cannot comprehend this.

104. The one is not, and the other one is, but they are united. This is He who shall not be able to come unto those who have a heart of flesh. (He is not here, but He exists. However, He cannot inhabit a heart of those who are attached to the fleshly world.)

105. Before you possess all knowledge, should you not know yourself? If you do not know yourself, how can you enjoy those things you have. Only those who have understood themselves shall enjoy the things they have come to possess.

106. The perfected person cannot be captured or seen. If they could

see him, they could capture him. The path to grace can only come from the perfect light. Unless one is clothed in the perfect light and it shows on and in him he shall not be able to come out from the World as the perfected son of the Bridal-Chamber. We must be perfected before we come out from the world. Whoever has received all before mastering all, will not be able to master the kingdom. He shall go to the transition (death) imperfect. Only Jesus knows his destiny.

107. The holy person is entirely holy, including his body. If one blesses the bread and sanctifies it, or the cup, or everything else he receives, why will he not sanctify the body also?

108. By perfecting the water of Baptism: thus Jesus washed away death. Because of this, we are descent into the water but not into death. We are not poured out into the wind (spirit) of the world. Whenever that blows, its winter has come. When the Holy Spirit breathes, summer has come.

109. Whoever recognizes the truth is set free. He who is set free does not go back (sin), for the one who goes back (the sinner) is the slave of sin. Truth is the Mother. When we unite with her it is recognition of the truth. Those who are set free from sin (no longer have to sin) are called free by the world. It is the recognition of the truth that exalts the hearts of those who are set free from sin. This is what liberates them and places them over the entire world. Love builds (inspires). He who is has been set free through this recognition is a slaved of love for those who have not yet set free by the truth.

Knowledge makes them capable of being set free. Love does not take anything selfishly. How can it when it possesses all thing? It does not say; "This is mine or that is mine", but it says: "All of this belongs to you."

110. Spiritual love is wine with fragrance. All those who are anointed with it enjoy it. Those who are near to the anointed ones enjoy it also. But when the anointed ones depart the bystanders who are not anointed remain in their own stench. The Samaritan gave nothing to the wounded man except wine and oil for anointing. The wounds were healed, for "love covers a multitude of sins."

111. The children of a women resemble the man who loves her. If the man is her husband, they resemble her husband. If the man is her illicit lover, they resemble him. Often, a woman will have sex with her husband out of duty but her heart is with her lover with whom she also has sex. The children of such a union often resemble the lover. You who live with the Son of God and do not also love the world but love the Lord only will have children that look like the Lord and not the world.

112. Humans mate with the humans, horses mate with horses, donkeys mate with donkeys; Like attracts like and they group together. Spirits unite with Spirits, and the thought (Word) mingles with the thought (Word), as Light merges with Light. If you become person then people will love you. If you become a spirit, then the Spirit shall merge with you. If thou become thought, then the thought

(Word) shall unite with you. If you become enlightened, then the Light shall merge with you. If you rise above this world, then that which is from above shall rest upon (in) you. But, if you become like a horse, donkey, bull, dog, sheep, or any other animal, domestic or feral, neither man nor Spirit nor Word (thought) nor the Light nor those from above nor those dwelling within shall be able to love you. They shall not be able to rest in you, and they will have no part in your inheritance to come.

113. He who is enslaved without his consent can be set free. He who has been set free by the grace of his master, but then sells himself back into slavery cannot be set free.

114. The cultivation in this world comes through four elements. Crops are harvested and taken into the barn only if there is first soil, water, wind, and light. God's harvest is also by means of four elements; faith (trust), hope (expectation), love (agape'), and knowledge (recognition of the truth). Our soil is the faith in which we take root. Our water is the hope by which we are nourished. Wind (spirit) is the love through which we grow. Light is the truth, which causes us to ripen. But, it is Grace that causes us to become kings of all heaven. Their souls are among the blessed for they live in Truth.

115. Jesus, the Christ, came to all of us but did not lay any burden on us. This kind of person is perfect and blessed. He is the Word of God. Ask us about him and we will tell you his righteousness is difficult to define or describe. A task so great assures failure.

116. How will he give rest to everyone; great or small, believer or not? He provides rest to all. There are those who attempt to gain by assisting the rich. Those who see themselves as rich are picky. They do not come of their own accord. Do not grieve them or anyone. It is natural to want to do good, but understand that the rich may seek to cause grief and he who seeks to do good could annoy those who think they are rich.

117. A householder had acquired everything. He had children, slaves, cattle, dogs, and pigs. He also had wheat, barley, straw, hay, meat, oil, and acorns. He was wise and knew what each needed to eat. He fed his children bread and meat. He fed the slaves oil with grain. The cattle were given barley straw and hay. The dogs received bones and the pigs got acorns and bread scraps. This is how it is with the disciple of God. If he is wise, he is understands discipleship. The bodily forms will not deceive him, but he will understand the condition of the souls around him. He will speak to each man on his own level. In the world there are many types of animals in human form. He must recognize each one. If the person is a pig, feed him acorns. If the person is a bull feed him barley with straw and hay; if a dog, throw him bones. If a person is a slave feed them basic food, but to the sons present the perfect and complete food.

118. There is the Son of Man and there is the son of the son of Man. The Lord is the Son of Man, and his son creates through him. God gave the Son of Man the power to create; he also gave him the ability to have children. That which is created is a creature. Those born are a

progeny (child / heir). A creature cannot propagate, but children can create. Yet they say that the creature procreates, however, the child is a creature. Therefore the creature's progeny are not his sons, but rather they are creations. He who creates works openly, and is visible. He who procreates does so in secret, and he hides himself from others. He who creates does so in open sight. He who procreates, makes his children (Son) in secret.

119. No one is able to know what day a husband and wife copulate. Only they know, because marriage in this world is a sacrament (mystery) for those who have taken a wife. If the act of an impure (common) marriage is hidden, the pure (immaculate) marriage is a deeper mystery (sacrament) and is hidden even more. It is not carnal (common) but it is pure (undefiled). it is not founded on lust. It is founded on true love (agape'). It is not part of the darkness or night. It is part of the light of. A marriage (act) which is seen (revealed / exposed) becomes vulgarity (common / prostitution), and the bride has played the whore not only if she has sex with another man, but also if she escapes from the bridle-chamber and is seen. She may only be seen (reveal herself to) by her father, her mother, (the friend of the bridegroom,) and the attendant of the bridegroom, and the bridegroom. Only these have permission go into the bridal-chamber on a daily basis. Others will yearn to hear her voice or enjoy her perfume (fragrance of the anointing oil). Let them be fed like dogs from the scraps that fall from the table. (Those) being from the Bridegroom with the Bride belong in the Bridal-Chamber. No one

will be able to see the Bridegroom or the Bride unless he becomes one like (with) them.

120. When Abraham was allowed (rejoiced at seeing what he was) to see, he circumcised the flesh of the foreskin to show us that it was correct (necessary) to renounce (kill) the flesh of this world.

121. As long as the entrails of a person are contained, the person lives and is well. If his entrails are exposed and he is disemboweled, the person will die. It is the same with a tree. If its roots are covered it will live and grow, but if its roots are exposed the tree will wither and die. It is the same with everything born into this world. It is the this way with everything manifest (seen) and covert (unseen). As long as the roots of evil are hidden, it is strong, but once evil it is exposed or recognized it is destroyed and it dies. This is why the Word says; "Already the ax has been laid to the root of the tree." It will not only chop down the tree, because that will permit it to sprout again, the ax will down into the ground and cleave the very root. Jesus uprooted what others had only partially cut down. Let each one of us dig deeply, down to the root of the evil that is within his heart and rip it out by its roots. If we can just recognize evil we can uproot it. However, if evil remains unrecognized, it will take root within us and yield its fruit in our hearts. It will make evil our master and we will be its slaves. Evil takes us captive, and coerces us into doing what we do not want to do. evil compels us into not doing what we should do. While it is unrecognized, it drives us .

122. Ignorance is the mother of all evil. Evil results in confusion and death. Truth is like ignorance. If it is hidden it rests within itself, but when it is revealed it is recognized and it is stronger that ignorance and error. Truth wins and liberates us from confusion. The Word said; "You shall know the truth and the truth shall set you free." Ignorance seeks to make us its slaves but knowledge is freedom. By recognizing the truth, we shall find the fruits of the truth within our hearts. If we join ourselves with the truth we shall be fulfilled.

123. Now, we have the visible (beings) things of creation and we say that visible things (beings) are the powerful and honorable, but the invisible things are the weak and unworthy of our attention. The nature of truth is different. In it, the visible things (beings) are weak and lowly, but the invisible are the powerful and honorable. The wisdom of the invisible God cannot be made known to us except that he takes visible form in ways we are accustomed to. Yet the mysteries of the truth are revealed, in types and symbols, but the bridle-chamber is hidden as it is with the holy of holies.

124. The veil of the Temple first concealed how God governed creation. Once the veil was torn and the things within (the Holy of Holies) were revealed, the house was to be forsaken, abandoned, and destroyed. Yet the entire Divinity (Godhead) was to depart, not to the holies of the holies, for it was not able to merge with the light nor unite with the complete fullness. It was to be under the wings of the cross, in its open arms. This is the ark which shall be salvation for us when the destruction of water has overwhelmed (overtaken) them.

125. Those in the priestly tribe shall be able to enter within the veil of the Temple along with the High Priest. This was symbolized by the fact that the veil was not torn at the top only, (but was torn from top to the bottom). If it was torn only at the top it would have been opened only for those who are on high (from the higher realm). If it were torn at the bottom only it would have been revealed only to those who are from below (the lower realm). But it was torn from the top to the bottom. Those who are from above made it available to us who are below them, so that we might enter into the secret of the truth. This strengthening of us is most wonderful. Because of this, we can enter in by means of symbols even though they are weak and worthless. They are humble and incomplete when compared to the perfect glory. It is the glory of glories and the power of powers. Through it the perfect is opened to us and it contains the secrets of the truth. Moreover, the holies of holies have been revealed and opened, and the bridle-chamber has invited us in.

126. As long as evil hidden, and not completely purged from among of the children of the Holy Spirit, it remains a potential threat. The children can be enslaved by the adversary, but when the Perfect Light is seen, it will pour out the oil of anointing upon within it, and the slaves shall be set free and the slaves shall be bought back.

127. Every plant not sown by my heavenly Father shall be pulled up by the root. Those who were estranged shall be united and empty shall be filled.

128. Everyone who enters the bridal-chamber shall ignite (be born in) the Light. This is like a marriages which takes place at night. The fire is ablaze and is seen in the dark but goes out before morning. The mysteries (sacraments) of the marriage are consummated in the light of day, and that light never dies.

129. If someone becomes a child of the Bridal-Chamber, he shall receive the Light. If one does not receive it in this place, he will not be able to receive it in any other place. He who has received that Light shall not be seen, nor captured. No one in the world will be able to disturb him. When he leaves the world he has will have already received the truth in types and symbols. The world has become eternity, because for him the fullness is eternal. It is revealed only to this kind of person. Truth is not hidden in darkness or the night. Truth is hidden in a perfect day and a holy light.

History of The Gospel Of Mary Magdalene

While traveling and researching is Cairo in 1896, German scholar, Dr. Carl Reinhardt, acquired a papyrus containing Coptic texts entitled the Revelation of John, the Wisdom of Jesus Christ, and the Gospel of Mary.

Before setting about to translate his exciting find two world wars ensued, delaying publication until 1955. By then the Nag Hammadi collection had also been discovered.

Two of the texts in his codex, the Revelation of John, and the Wisdom of Jesus Christ, were included there. Importantly, the codex preserves the most complete surviving copy of the Gospel of Mary, named for its supposed author, Mary of Magdala. Two other fragments of the Gospel of Mary written in Greek were later unearthed in archaelogical digs at Oxyrhynchus in Northern Egypt.

All of the various fragments were brought together to form the translation presented here. However, even with all of the fragments assembled, the manuscript of the Gospel of Mary is missing pages 1 to 6 and pages 11 to 14. These pages included sections of the text up to chapter 4, and portions of chapter 5 to 8.

Although the text of the Gospel of Mary is incomplete, the text presented below serves to shake the very concept of our assumptions of early Christianity as well as Christ's possible relationship to Mary of Magdala, whom we call Mary Magdalene.

The Gospel of Mary Magdalene

(Pages 1 to 6 of the manuscript, containing chapters 1 - 3, are lost. The extant text starts on page 7...)

Chapter 4

21 (And they asked Jesus), "Will matter then be destroyed or not?"

22) The Savior said; "All nature, all things formed, and all creatures exist in and with one another, and they will be desolved again into their own elements (origins).

23) This is because it is the nature of matter to return to its original elements.

24) If you have an ear to hear, listen to this.

25) Peter said to him; "Since you have explained all things to us, tell us this also: What sin did the world commit (what sin is in the world)?

26) The Savior said; "There is no sin (of the world). Each person makes his own sin when he does things like adultery (in the same nature as adultery). This is called sin.

27) That is why the Good came to be among you. He came to restore every nature to its basic root.

28) Then He continued; "You become sick and die because you did not have access to He who can heal you."

29) If you have any sense, you must understand this.

30) The material world produced a great passion (desire / suffering) without equal. This was contrary to the natural balance. The entire body was disturbed by it.

31) That is why I said to you; "Be encouraged, and if you are discouraged be encouraged when you see the different forms nature has taken.

32) He who has ears to hear, let him hear.

33) When the Blessed One had said this, He greeted them all of them and said; "Peace be with you. Take my peace into you.

34) Beware that no one deceives you by saying Look (he is) here or look (he is) there. The Son of Man is within you.

35) Follow Him there.

36) Those who seek Him will find Him.

37) Go now and preach the gospel of the Kingdom.

38) Do not lay down any rules beyond what I appointed you, and do not give a law like the lawgivers (Pharisee) or you will be held to account for the same laws.

39) When He said this He departed.

Chapter 5

1) Then they were troubled and wept out loud, saying, How shall we go to the Gentiles and preach the gospel of the Kingdom of the Son of Man? If they did not spare Him, how can we expect that they will spare us?

2) Then Mary stood up, greeted them all, and said to her follow believers, "Do not weep and do not be troubled and do not waver, because His grace will be with you completely and it will protect you.

3) Instead, let us praise His greatness, because He has prepared us and made us into mature (finished / complete) people.

4) Mary's words turned their hearts to the Good, and they began to discuss the words of the Savior.

5) Peter said to Mary; "Sister we know that the Savior loved you more than all other woman.

6) Tell us the words of the Savior that you remember and know, but have we heard and do not know.

7) Mary answered him and said; "I will tell you what He hid from you."

8) And she began to speak these words to them; "She said, I saw the Lord in a vision and I said to Him, 'Lord I saw you today in a vision.'

9) He answered and said to me; "You will be happy that you did not waver at the sight of Me. Where the mind is there is the treasure.

10) I said to Him; "Lord, does one see visions through the soul or through the spirit?"

11) The Savior answered and said; "He sees visions through neither the soul nor the spirit. It is through the mind that is between the two. That is what sees the vision and it is (there the vision exists.)

(pages 11 - 14 are missing from the manuscript)

Chapter 8:

10) And desire (a lesser god) said; "Before, I did not see you descending, but now I see you ascending. Why do you lie since you belong to me?"

11) The soul answered and said; "I saw you but you did not see me nor recognize me. I covered you like a garment and you did not know me.

12) When it said this, the soul went away greatly rejoicing.

13) Again it came to the third power (lesser god), which is called ignorance.

14) The power questioned the soul, saying, Where are you going? You are enslaved (captured) in wickedness. Since you are its captive you cannot judge (have no judgment).

15) And the soul said: "Why do you judge me, when I have not judged?

16) I was captured, although I have not captured anyone.

17) I was not recognized. But I have recognized that God (the All) is in (being dissolved), both the earthly things and the heavenly.

18) When the soul had overcome the third power, it ascended and saw the fourth power, which took seven forms.

19) The first form is darkness, the second desire, the third ignorance, the fourth is the lust of death, the fifth is the dominion of the flesh, the sixth is the empty useless wisdom of flesh, the seventh is the wisdom of vengeance and anger. These are the seven powers of wrath.

20) They asked the soul; "Where do you come from, slayer of men, where are you going, conqueror of space?"

21) The soul answered and said; "What has trapped me has been slain, and what kept me caged has been overcome,

22) My desire has been ended, and ignorance has died.

23) In an age (dispensation) I was released from the world in a symbolic image, and I was released from the chains of oblivion, which were only temporary (in this transient world).

24) From this time on will I attain the rest of the ages and seasons of silence.

Chapter 9

1) When Mary had said this, she fell silent, since she had shared all the Savior had told her.

2) But Andrew said to the other believers; "Say what you want about what she has said, but I do not believe that the Savior said this. These teachings are very strange ideas.

3) Peter answered him and spoke concerning these things.

4) He questioned them about the Savior and asked; "Did He really speak privately with a woman and not openly to us? Are we to turn around and all listen to her? Did He prefer her to us?"

5) Then Mary sobbed and said to Peter; "My brother Peter, what do you think? Do you think that I have made all of this up in my heart by myself? Do you think that I am lying about the Savior?"

6) Levi said to Peter; "Peter you have always had a hot temper."

7) Now I see you fighting against this woman like she was your enemy.

8) If the Savior made her worthy, who are you to reject her? What do you think you are doing? Surely the Savior knows her well?

9) That is why He loved her more than us. Let us be ashamed out this and let us put on the perfect Man. Let us separate from each other as He commanded us to do so we can preach the gospel, not laying down any other rule or other law beyond what the Savior told us.'

10) And when they heard this they began to go out and proclaim and preach.

Didache

History and Introduction

Didache" (pronounced "dih-dah-KAY" or "didah-KEY") is the Greek word meaning "teaching" or "doctrine".

The book, *"The Didache"* is also called *"The Teaching of the Twelve Apostles."* It is a treatise, consisting of sixteen short chapters that dates back to the earliest time of the Christian Church and was considered by some of the Church Fathers to be almost as important as the Holy Scriptures.

The Didache reveals how the Christians of the first century operated on a day-to-day basis. It is not a gospel and it does not attempt to offer guidance by narrating the life of Jesus. In fact, some of the theology it contains runs counter to the modern interpretation of the theology in the received gospels.

The Didache represents the first concerted effort put forth by church leaders to teach the common person of the early church how to live and worship in the way that the apostles of Jesus presented to their followers. This was the way of a Jewish Christian.

The Didache describes a way in which Gentiles and pagans could be converted, initiated, and brought into the fold to become full participants in a shared Christian life. This unity of process and teaching allowed a community, which believed itself to be poised on the threshold of the end times, to fashion its daily life in order to share the passion of the awaited return of the Kingdom of God as preached by Jesus. In fact, it is the first known instruction manual for Christian converts.

There is evidence of its use specifically by Nazarene synagogues to define and standardize the most important points of the new faith. Nazarenes were Jews who converted to a sect following Jesus. They were Hellenized Jews on the Syrian border close to Antioch.

Certainly, the Didache was used by Jewish Christians but as Paul influenced the Nazarenes (a sect of which he was thought to be a leader), his followers diverged from the theology in the Didache. The "Pauline Christians" evolved into a separate sect leaving behind the Didache.

The Didache appears to be an "evolved" document, meaning it has been edited, altered, or expanded over time as the early church grew and changed. There are style changes indicating the document was the creation of more than one person.

The section of the Didache titled, "There Are Two Ways," is the name of an older Jewish document and the first section of the Didache that was amended and used by several early Christian communities.

This duality of presentation is also echoed in the Shepherd of Hermas and the Epistle of Barnabas. The middle two sections of the Didache may be a bit older than the first section.

The Didache was discovered in 1873 by Philotheos Bryennios, Metropolitan of Nicomedia, in a small eleventh century codex of 120 pages. He published the text toward the end of 1883. The Didache has been the center of much academic interest and controversy since its discovery. Prior to this time its existence was known only through references by early writers. It was thought the text was lost to history.

Church fathers including Athanasius, Rufinus, and John of Damascas cited the book as inspired scripture and thus made us aware of the text. The Didache was also accepted into the Apostolic Constitutions Canon, which was written between 250-380 C.E. This compilation of eight books describes administrative canons for the clergy and the laity along with guides for worship. The books were supposed to be works of the apostles, but actually included the greater part of the *Didascalia Apostolorum,* a lost Greek treatise of 3rd century origin, along with most of the Didache, and fragments from Hippolytus and Papias. The work concludes with a collection of 85 moral and liturgical canons known as the "Apostolic Canons," a portion of which became part of canon law of the Western Church. The work is thought to be of Syrian origin. As is the Didache. This document is also a valuable primary source on early church history and practice. It is not nearly as early a text as the Didache however.

The Didache is incorporated into a larger book which is used as part of the 81-book Ethiopic Canon. The Didache has been known in an extended Ethiopic version, called the Didascalia, which is actually part of the extended New Testament canon of the Ethiopian Orthodox Church. Many early church fathers including Barnabas, Irenaeus, Clement of Alexandria, and Origen either quote or reference the Didache.

The Didache has raised great controversy regarding its date and possible origin. Some scholars dated the text between approximately 49-79 AD. Although this is widely debated it could place the Didache as one of the oldest Christian writings in history and written before three of the Gospels, if not all of the Gospels.

Even though the Didache has been changed and added to over time there is strong evidence to suggest that the earliest section of it may have been penned during the time of the Jerusalem Council, around 50 AD. This would have it playing a role in the early church's controversy surrounding salvation of the Gentiles as described in the Book of Acts (ca. 50 – 100 C.E with many saying 62-64 C.E.) chapter 15.

Acts 15

New International Version (NIV)

The Council at Jerusalem

1 Certain people came down from Judea to Antioch and were teaching the believers: "Unless you are circumcised, according to the custom taught by Moses, you cannot be saved." 2 This brought Paul and Barnabas into sharp dispute and debate with them. So Paul and Barnabas were appointed, along with some other believers, to go up to Jerusalem to see the apostles and elders about this question. 3 The church sent them on their way, and as they traveled through Phoenicia and Samaria, they told how the Gentiles had been converted. This news made all the believers very glad. 4 When they came to Jerusalem, they were welcomed by the church and the apostles and elders, to whom they reported everything God had done through them. 5 Then some of the believers who belonged to the party of the Pharisees stood up and said, "The Gentiles must be circumcised and required to keep the law of Moses." 6 The apostles and elders met to consider this question. 7 After much discussion, Peter got up and addressed them: "Brothers, you know that some time ago God made a choice among you that the Gentiles might hear from my lips the message of the gospel and believe. 8 God, who knows the heart, showed that he accepted them by giving the Holy Spirit to them, just as he did to us. 9 He did not discriminate between us and them, for he purified their hearts by faith. 10 Now then, why do you try to test God by putting on the necks of Gentiles a yoke that neither we nor our ancestors have been able to bear? 11 No! We believe it is through the grace of our Lord Jesus that we are saved, just as they are."

12 The whole assembly became silent as they listened to Barnabas and Paul telling about the signs and wonders God had done among the Gentiles through them. 13 When they finished, James spoke up. "Brothers," he said, "listen to me. 14 Simon has described to us how God first intervened to choose a people for his name from the Gentiles. 15 The words of the prophets are in agreement with this, as it is written: 16 "'After this I will return and rebuild David's fallen tent. Its ruins I will rebuild, and I will restore it, 17 that the rest of mankind may seek the Lord, even all the Gentiles who bear my name, says the Lord, who does these things'— 18 things known from long ago. 19 "It is my judgment, therefore, that we should not make it difficult for the Gentiles who are turning to God. 20 Instead we should write to them, telling them to abstain from food polluted by idols, from sexual immorality, from the meat of strangled animals and from blood. 21 For the law of Moses has been preached in every city from the earliest times and is read in the synagogues on every Sabbath." 22 Then the apostles and elders, with the whole church, decided to choose some of their own men and send them to Antioch with Paul and Barnabas. They chose Judas (called Barsabbas) and Silas, men who were leaders among the believers. 23 With them they sent the following letter: The apostles and elders, your brothers, To the Gentile believers in Antioch, Syria and Cilicia: Greetings. 24 We have heard that some went out from us without our authorization and disturbed you, troubling your minds by what they said. 25 So we all agreed to choose some men and send them to you with our dear friends Barnabas and Paul— 26 men who have risked their lives for the name of our Lord Jesus Christ. 27 Therefore we are sending Judas and Silas to confirm by word of mouth what we are writing. 28 It seemed good to the Holy Spirit and to us not to burden you with anything beyond the following requirements: 29 You are to abstain from food sacrificed to idols, from blood, from the meat of strangled animals and from sexual immorality. You will do well to avoid these things.

Farewell. 30 So the men were sent off and went down to Antioch, where they gathered the church together and delivered the letter. 31 The people read it and were glad for its encouraging message. 32 Judas and Silas, who themselves were prophets, said much to encourage and strengthen the believers. 33 After spending some time there, they were sent off by the believers with the blessing of peace to return to those who had sent them. 34- 35 But Paul and Barnabas remained in Antioch, where they and many others taught and preached the word of the Lord.

Here, in the book of Acts, the apostles began to set a pattern that only a small list of the law needed to be kept, but the law as a whole was put aside. How much of that law that needs to be fulfilled became a point of contention. (The Pharisees mentioned in Act 5 were Christians.)

For the discussion within Acts to take place it must be before 64 C.E. Margherita Guarducci, who led the research leading to the rediscovery of Peter's tomb in its last stages (1963–1968), concludes

Peter died on 13 October AD 64 during the festivities on the occasion of the "dies imperii" of Emperor Nero. This took place three months after the disastrous fire that destroyed Rome for which the emperor blamed the Christians. This "dies imperii" (regnal day anniversary) was an important one, exactly ten years after Nero ascended to the throne, and it was accompanied by much bloodshed.

Traditionally, Roman authorities sentenced Peter to death by crucifixion. According to the apocryphal Acts of Peter, he was crucified head down, thinking himself unworthy to die as Jesus Died. Tradition also locates his burial place where the Basilica of Saint Peter was later built, directly beneath the Basilica's high altar.

Clement of Rome, in his Letter to the Corinthians (Chapter 5), written c. 80–98, speaks of Peter's martyrdom in the following terms: "Let us take the noble examples of our own generation. Through jealousy and envy the greatest and most just pillars of the Church were persecuted, and came even unto death… Peter, through unjust envy, endured not one or two but many labors, and at last, having delivered his testimony, departed unto the place of glory due to him."

In Rome, Christians were being hunted down. Soon, in Jerusalem Jews would be killed by the hundreds of thousands. James was killed in 62 or 69 C.E. Yet, it is my contention that Jewish Christians were targeted with greater accuracy, given the ease of recognizing them in Synagogues. Gentile Christians could hide amongst the Roman population.

To place things in perspective, here are the ranges of dates that encompass the writing of the earliest gospels. These are the currently accepted dates from the earliest by the more religious scholars to the latest more liberal or secular scholars:

Matthew: 37 to 100 C.E.
Mark: 40 to 73 C.E.
Luke: 50 to 100 C.E.
John: 65 to 100 C.E.

The earliest dates are based on the events recounted in the gospels themselves. The mention of the destruction of the Jerusalem temple, which occurred in 70 C.E. is usually used as a point of reference.

According to this scholarship, the gospels must have been written after the devastation because they refer to it. Conservative believers maintain the early dates demonstrate Jesus' divine powers of prophecy. They believe the Gospels were written earlier.

The Didache may have been written before Matthew, and certainly before Acts (62 – 100 C.E.). When one looks at the discussion between the apostles regarding the law and the Gentiles in Acts it appears James, the leader, either changed his mind about keeping the Laws of Moses or was faced with the mass conversion of Gentiles as a new phenomenon. This evolution of insight was due to the fact God saved Gentiles who were not keeping the laws did not change the message from the Jewish leaders as to who Jesus was and what his mission was, to the Jews and now to the Gentiles. Even though the Gentiles need not keep the law, they must express their faith through a set of actions.

The placement of the Didache in history can be based on the following facts:

• When it was written, churches were still being led by traveling teachers and prophets.

• In its instructions on the appointment of church leaders, it mentions only two classes: bishops and deacons.

• Baptisms are still normally performed in rivers and streams.

• Prophets still preside at the Eucharist.

• The Eucharist or communion is still celebrated in conjunction with the agape or love feast.

• The absence of any theological dogma or discussion.

The range is wide in the speculation of the dates for the Didache, between 50 and 100 C.E.

There are clues that the author (or authors) of the Didache were close to either Jesus, or possibly the understudy of an Apostle. The author clearly shared in Jesus' opinion of the Pharisees as hypocrites (8:1). The author also had intimate knowledge of the Gospel of Matthew, or the "Q" source.

No intact copy of "Q" has ever been found. No reference to the document in early Christian writings has survived. Its existence is inferred from an analysis of the text of Matthew and Luke. Much of the content of Matthew and Luke was derived from the Gospel of Mark. But there were also many passages which appear to have come from another source document called the "Q" document.

Theologians and religious historians believe the Q's text can be reconstructed by analyzing passages that Matthew and Luke have in common. "Q" had to be written much earlier than the four canonical gospels of Mark, Matthew, Luke and John since there are identical passages in Mathew and Luke supplied by "Q". It may have been in the first of the 40 or so Gospels that were written and used by the early Christian movements before the controlling faction established what was to be orthodoxy and selected the books which were to become canon.

The Gospel of Q is different from the canonical gospels in that it does not extensively describe events in the life of Jesus. Rather, it is largely a collection of sayings -- similar to the Gospel of Thomas (see "the Gospel of Thomas by Joseph Lumpkin, published by Fifth Estate). Q does not mention the events of Jesus' virgin birth, his selection of 12 disciples, crucifixion, resurrection, or ascension to heaven. It represents those parts of Jesus' teachings that his followers remembered and recorded about 20 years after his death. Jesus is presented as a charismatic teacher, a healer, a simple man filled with the spirit of God. Jesus is also a sage, the personification of Wisdom, and the servant of God.

Through analysis of Matthew and Luke it is possible to draw out those verses that are identical, word for word, suggesting it was not an oral tradition or anything done from memory, it was a written source used for both. This document of "Q" can be found in Appendix "C" of this book.

By putting together the Didache and "Q" we have a view of the gospel and the doctrine of the young church and a glimpse into the heart of the first Christians.

The earliest Christian preaching about Jesus concerned his death and resurrection. It was only later that the early Church turned its attention to the chronology and events of the rest of the life of Jesus.

It was the resurrection that was the most important event in Christianity, especially for the earliest Christians. The resurrection was God's stamp of approval on the messiah. It was the power of God coming upon his good and faithful servant that raised him up as a sign for the people that this was indeed the real anointed one, the real Christ, the real messiah. The resurrection left no doubt.

Early Christians were hardly monolithic in their preachings and it was not until the 2nd century C.E. that the concept of the virgin birth of Jesus took hold. Critics of the virgin birth claim the concept was taken from pagan religions such as Mithaism, a mystery religion practiced in Rome between the first and fourth centuries C.E. Other critics claim the virgin birth was a counter claim to the Jewish slander of the illegitimate birth of Jesus. However, since both Matthew and Luke attest to the event it is supported by two witnesses, but this is only two of the four gospels. Such a miraculous event would likely be recorded by all.

There is speculation the Didache is a collaborative work of some council members as a proposed draft for the letter finally sent to outline under what conditions and through what teaching and by what initiation could a Gentile become a Christian (Acts 15:22-29). James would have been the main contributor as the leader. This seems to be supported by the key points made in Chapters 1-6, which elaborate on the more simplified points that were made in the final letter. Some instruction (4:8, 6:3, 8:8) also appears to overlap with events in early chapters of Acts, and there is also some terminology used during the time of Acts, such as *your servant, Jesus* (9:3, 9:5, 10:3), and one use of the term *Christian* (12:4). The letter would have gone out immediately while Acts would have been penned later.

The Didache falls into three parts. The first part (Chapters 1-6) is a moral treatise describing the Two Ways, the Way of Life and the Way of Death. The second and third parts contain instructions on baptism, the Eucharist, fasting, prayer, matters of church organization for the positions of apostles, teachers, prophets, bishops, and deacons.

It is perhaps the first text to append a doxology to the Lord's Prayer "...for thine is the power and the glory unto all ages." This doxology was picked up by the church and is now part of the Lord's Prayer for the Protestant churches. The words "the kingdom" were added later and are preserved in the document "The Apostolic Constitutions". The Textus Receptus, from which the King James Version was translated, included many references to a "didache" or teaching of the apostles, and several quotes from the didache, such as the longer version of the Lord's Prayer.

The "Our Father" is contained twice in the Bible (Matt. 6:9-13; Luke 11:2-4) with no doxology. In fact no doxology is found in the older manuscripts. The doxology is simply a prayer from the believers whose spirits were moved to close the prayer with deep reverence.

The normal practice in Judaism was for the person praying to add his own requests and doxology to a prayer that did not already have a fixed conclusion. The fact that the Lord's Prayer ends abruptly explains why early Jewish Christians may have felt the prayer required a personal conclusion. Tertullian confirms that in his day the practice was for worshippers to append their own petitions to the Lord's Prayer.

221

Egypt and Syria both have claims as the place of origin for the Didache. The case for Egypt was put forward because Clement of Alexandria, an early witness, stated it was very popular in Egypt, in the fourth century. He based this on Anthanasius The Great's reference to it and the numerous Coptic and Ethiopian versions available. The case for Syria is in the text on ministry and the apostolic decree of Acts 15:23-9 describing characteristic of early Syrian Christianity. The text in chapter 6 suggests a large but rural community, like that of Syria rather than the more metropolitan Egypt.

The Didache should not be confused with the *"Didascalia Apostolorum"*, *"Teaching of the Twelve Holy Apostles and Disciples of Our Savior,"* a 3rd century text founded upon the *Didache. The Didache* is the foundation of the Didascalia, which is an expanded version of the Didache. The Didascalia continues to be part of the canon of the Ethiopic Christian church called the "Broader Canon."

The Didache is the earliest Orthodox Christian writing we have that is not contained in the New Testament and likely predates most of the writings contained in the New Testament.

Because it predates so much of the New Testament, it predates the idea of Sola Scriptura, the idea that the Bible contains all knowledge needed for salvation. Not only was Sola Scriptura unknown, it would have been impossible. There was no New Testament to point to as scripture. No Scriptura - no Sola Scriptura.

The Didache is a witness to the early Church of the Apostolic Age, and is evidence that the Faith of the Orthodox Church today is much the same as that of Christians of those times.

The original is a composite text. One of the earliest copies is known as the Jerusalem manuscript. It seems to be a reliable copy and was written at the close of the first century. If it is a culmination of the evolutionary process, then the texts or ideas backing this text must have emerged earlier. This would put the date of the ideas so far back as to coincide with the period of the earliest Jewish converts to the sect of the Nazarene.

The texts have evolved over a considerable period, from its beginning as a Jewish catechetical work, which was taken up and developed by the Church into a manual of Church life and order. The text was repeatedly modified in line with changes in the practice of the people of the communities who used it. The core of chapters 1 - 6 is Jewish and pre-Christian (ca. 100 B.C.E. to 50 C.E.) but this is to be expected since early Christianity was a sect of Judaism and thus followed basic Jewish religious practices. As a whole the text reached its present form by the end of the first century C.E.

There exists an eleventh century manuscript bearing the names "The Didache" and "The Teaching of the Twelve Apostles" ("Didache ton dodeka apostolon"). These are not the same texts, although the latter is an expansion of the first.

The Jerusalem manuscript was discovered in 1873 by Greek Orthodox Archbishop Philotheos Bryennios, Metropolitan of Nicomedia, in the library of the patriarch of Jerusalem at Constantinople. It is a clear and accurate copy made by a man called Leo, "scribe & sinner", dated to the year 1056 C.E. In 1883, Byrennios translated the manuscript, with introduction and comments. He correctly identified the Didache as the product of a Jewish Christian community.

A couple of years later, an Ethiopian version of the Didache was found and then published by Horner in 1904. Greek & Coptic fragments were discovered among the Oxyrhynchus Papyri. In 1992 the Greek version was published, followed by the Coptic version in 1924.

The Greek version of the Didache is contained in Appendix "B" of this book.

The text as we have it today can be divided into four evolutionary phases:

(1) the original text (ca. 50-100 C.E.) : the first century original;
(2) the composite versions of the text in view of the needs of a particular Jewish Christian community ;

(3) the oldest extant independent & complete MS of such a composite version : the Jerusalem MS is a 1056 copy and bears two titles. The text has a composition that does not flow, as it shifts from the writing style of one person to another, but it has a unity of the composition. It is clearly the product of a joint effort, containing mid second century additions or changes;

(4) the critical text : 21th century translation and interpretation with consideration given to all known documents, such as the Jerusalem MS, the Latin and Ethiopian versions and the Greek and Coptic fragments.

Harnack argues that the completed Didache originated in a backward community in rural Egypt around 140-165 C.E., whereas Sabatier claims a mid first century redaction (or earlier), in Syria. Recently, Mack situated the text in Galilea, about 100 C.E. Others claim 50 – 100 C.E. Hence, the precise date and place of origin of the original text remains a matter of debate, although a first century original is very likely. Judging from the form of the prayers and how they follow Jewish customs, the text must have been written in the time before pagan followers and influences began to be introduced, and well before the time when Christianity began to diverge from its Jewish roots.

There is a dualistic approach to logic and teaching in the text. Even though this is seen in Old Testament books such as Proverbs the approach in the Didache is not the short, two sentence type found there but more of the dualism or binary logic taught by the Greeks. There is no reason to think that the form of the Two Ways tradition shared by Barnabas and the Didache were from Semitic Judaism. The form seems more the type that flourished in the Greek schools of Hellenistic Judaism and philosophy for decades, if not centuries. Early Christian writers later came to adopt it. Two Ways theme in the Didache is almost exclusively limited to Didache 1.1-6.2. The Two Way approach is absent from Didache 6.3-15.4. This shows evidence of additions and evolutions.

It is possible that some connection once existed between the Didache and a Two Ways tradition presented in Barnabas. Some material present in the Two Ways can also be seen in Hermas, Similitudes 9.26.3. It is difficult to say with certainty which came first, but it is likely that Barnabas borrowed freely from the approach or presentation style of the Didache.

The strong Jewish influence, emphasis on leadership, prophecy, baptism and liturgies based around the Eucharistic along with the belief in the immediate return of Jesus Christ as the foundation of spiritual and communal life all imply that it was part of the earliest stage of the development of the myth of Christ, which apparently set in very rapidly after Jesus died or departed.

If the original, or core text was written before 100 C.E. but after the destruction of the second Temple in 70 C.E. it would situate the original Didache in the period of 70-100 C.E. The text contains material pertaining to first century Jewish concepts and its "two way" morality, which point to the Qumran community and the earliest forms of "Christianity" with what we now recognize as baptism and thanksgiving. However, since we know the Qumran community was in place a century before, and was an apocalyptic sect it is no proof of date.

There is a reference to "the Name of the Father, the Son and the Holy Spirit" in the ceremony of baptism, but the place and purpose of each "member" is not defined. The formula for baptism should not be read as Trinitarian since the divinity of Jesus was not accepted by most Jews, even some Christian Jews. It is probably a later interpolation placed upon the text. Nowhere else is the "Son" invoked (except in His apocalyptic station - 16:4), and nowhere is the identity of Jesus as the "Son of God" clearly and explicitly made.

The Didache, together with the epistles, were read during worship by the sect called Judeo-Christians. It was often cited by the Church Fathers. Some of them placed it next to the New Testament. As an overview of the major points, let us look at Baptism, Fasting, and the Eucharist.

Baptism:

"But concerning baptism, thus shall ye baptize. Having first recited all these things, baptize in the name of the Father and of the Son and of the Holy Spirit in living [running] water. But if thou hast not living water, then baptize in other water; and if thou art not able in cold, then in warm. But if thou hast neither, then pour water on the head thrice in the name of the Father and of the Son and of the Holy Spirit. But before the baptism let him that baptizes and him that is baptized fast, and any others also who are able; and thou shalt order him that is baptized to fast a day or two before." - Didache, 7:1-7

The early Christian practices of Baptism via triple immersion and fasting before Baptism are still preserved in the Orthodox Church today.

Fasting:

"And let not your fastings be with the hypocrites [Jews], for they fast on the second [Monday] and the fifth [Thursday] day of the week; but do ye keep your fast on the fourth [Wednesday] and on the preparation [the sixth -- Friday] day." - Didache, 8:1-2

Eucharist:

"But let no one eat or drink of this eucharistic thanksgiving, but they that have been baptized into the name of the Lord; for concerning this also the Lord hath said: Give not that which is holy to the dogs." Didache, 9:10-12

The Didache has many similarities to other epistles written around the same time. These epistles are:

1st Epistle of Clement to the Corinthians (ca. 96) is a formal letter sent by the church of Rome to the church of Corinth as a result of trouble there that had led to the disposition of presbyters. Clement urges the Christians of Corinth (rebelling against church authority) to be submissive and obedient. Tradition attributes it to Clement, the first bishop of Rome who claimed catholic authority.

The Epistle of Barnabas (ca. 130) is a letter written to repudiate the claims of Jewish Christians who advocated adhering to the observance of the Law of Moses.

The Shepherd of Hermas (ca. 150) is an apocalyptic text written by Hermas, who is believed to be brother of Pius, the bishop of Rome. Practical matters of church purity and discipline in the second century come to the fore.

The Epistle of Polycarp to the Philippians (ca. 130) was a church leader (bishop) in Smyrna, Asia Minor. He exhorted the Philippians to holy living, good works and unmovable faith. He was interested in ministry and practical aspects of the daily life of Christians.

The Martyrdom of Polycarp is the earliest preserved story of Christian martyrs, probably from the last part of the second century. It records the trial and execution of Polycarp, who was burned at the stake.

The writings of Ignatius, who was the bishop of Antioch in Syria martyred in Rome by beasts in the beginning of the second century. On his way to Rome, he visited and then wrote to various churches, warning and exhorting them. He also wrote to Rome, and to Polycarp, bishop of Smyrna. He warned the church against heresies that threatened peace and unity, opposed Gnosticism and Docetism. He penned letters to the Ephesians, Magnesians, Trallians, Romans, Philadelphians, Smyrnaeans and a letter to Polycarp.

In a time when Jewish Christianity was less refined and organized and followers were faced with defining the major elements of the emergent Christian faith it was the Didache that offered the first text book of worship. Importance is given to the way of life, to prophecy, to communal gatherings, to the apocalypse, and to the soon return of Jesus.

"Jesus Christ" is only mentioned once, during the rite of broken bread (9:3-4). The sharing of eucharistic bread is not the reason for the gathering. There is no mention of the one body of Christ (1 Corinthians, 10:17). The breaking of bread is a foretaste and anticipation of the return of Christ and the perfection of self and community his return will bring, when all are united, and the "end time" brings restoration of holiness, peace, and complete harmony with God and His followers.

Christ is not mentioned during the rite of cup (9:2), neither does this title appear in the communal thanksgiving prayer, which is offered after the meal.

During the eucharist (9:2-3, 10:2-3) Jesus is called "servant" (Greek "pais") of the Father and "Christ" (annionted) only once and his connection with the "broken bread" is referenced in 9:4.

The early Christian community believed the beginning of the "end time" and the coming apocalypse was heralded with the arrival and death of Jesus. It is the space of time between then and the return of Jesus that we deal with here.

In the Didache, the traditional Jewish custom of drinking wine, breaking bread and saying thanks after the meal was not made referring to Christ nor was the meal or thanksgiving looking to the relationship between bread and wine and the Body and Blood of the "Son of God". The love-meal (agape) was rooted in the eucharist but became isolated only after the ritual meal of Judaism and the eucharist were separated. At the time there were many pagan religions conducting rituals in which there was symbolic eating of the "flesh" of a sacrificial victim or "god". The ceremony was common throughout the Middle East with the mystery cults, Mithraism, Isis and Osiris, Greek mysteries and other religious festivals. The rituals proposed in the Didache are not about this pagan practice but are firmly rooted in the tradition of Jewish prayer and community.

Didache 10 is suggestive of the "birkat ha-mazon", a thanksgiving prayer at the end of the Jewish supper.

There is no mention that Christ is god who came in the flesh and died on the cross for our sins. This notion became the basis for the Christian Mass later.

(It should be noted, as odd as it may seem to modern Christians, that there were those who believed that Jesus was born of a virgin but still rejected his divinity. One idea does not follow the other.)

The disagreement between Eastern and Western Christianity as to the precise moment that consecration of the host happens within the Mass (both positions being without empirical proof) caused a schism between Eastern and Western Christianity. The West believes at the mention of "the Son" there is consecration (and transubstantiation), whereas the East invokes the Holy Spirit to effect the change of the substances of the Eucharist.

There are traces of Q-material in the Didache, which indicates that the Didache is independent of the seed document Matthew and Luke drew upon, which most believe was the Gospel of Mark, or the notes and traditions which gave rise to Mark. Perhaps the Didache helps to explain the background behind the gospel texts. The Didache suggests an independence from the synoptic Gospels and so throws light on the text of these gospels. This may confirm that the sayings of Jesus were collected in a written form. These may be the saying which were later placed into a document of over one hundred sayings of Jesus called, "The Gospel of Thomas." Like the Didache, the Gospel of Thomas is not a narrative gospel but a wisdom discourse.

The information within the text is presented as a wisdom book based on the sayings of Jesus, which is in the Q document, instead of the narrative gospels, which tell a story. There is a parallel between Didache 9:5 where a logia is mentioned and the Gospel of Thomas.

If we examine what became the Lord's Prayer we find it fairly intact.
"When you pray, say :
'Father, may Your Name be holy.
May Your rule take place.
Always give us our bread.
Forgive us our debts,
for we ourselves forgive everyone that is indebted to us.
And lead us away from a trying situation'."
Q1, logia 42-44.

The word "epiousios" (8:2) is usually translated as "daily". This translation is somewhat arbitrary but became ubiquitous and thus the accepted rendering. The word "epiousion" has "epi" and "ousia as its parts. Epi means, "it is present" or "it happens". "Ousia" means "substance or essence". It refers to the "bread". If "epiousion" is understood as a "spiritual" process happening with the bread, then this word can be read as, "Give us now our spiritual bread."

The early Christians believed that Christ would come back within their lifetime. Their liturgies served to remind them of the imminent return. The love feast or Eucharist was not part of His death as it is today. There was no interpretation of "bread" as the "Body of Christ", nor is there a trace of the "this is My body" - "this is My blood". The meal - the Eucharist - was a gathering and a meal as a rehearsal and reminder of what communal unity and love was to come. To experience the presence of Christ by anticipating his return is evidenced in the Didache. This is the only text we have containing liturgical information about the Q-communities, of which the Essenes belonged.

The Didache shows little to no "Pauline" Christianity. Paul would have been present but his influence had not yet been fully established. It was James, the brother of Jesus, who was the "heir apparent" after the death of Jesus. James headed the Jewish Christian movement. Although Peter may have had a high status it was James who became the head of the Christian church or ministry in Jerusalem, which was considered the holiest position at the time. James wished to continue closer to the line of Judaism but Paul wished to reach out to the Pagan Gentile population. Later, the Catholic Church would view Peter as the apostle of succession and attempt to trace the papal lineage back to him, however Paul, it seems, had the greatest influence on

Christianity and much of our faith today is Christianity as interpreted by Paul.

Before Paul – Before the Epistles – Beofe the influx of gentiles – What did "Christians" think about their leader and who did they think he was? What did they practice? How did they worship and act? Let us read and see.

The Didache

(Roberts-Donaldson Translation)

The Lord's Teaching Through the Twelve Apostles to the Nations.

Chapter 1.

The Two Ways and the First Commandment. There are two ways, one of life and one of death, but a great difference between the two ways. The way of life, then, is this: First, you shall love God who made you; second, love your neighbor as yourself, and do not do to another what you would not want done to you. And of these sayings the teaching is this: Bless those who curse you, and pray for your enemies, and fast for those who persecute you. For what reward is there for loving those who love you? Do not the Gentiles do the same? But love those who hate you, and you shall not have an enemy. Abstain from fleshly and worldly lusts. If someone strikes your right cheek, turn to him the other also, and you shall be perfect. If someone impresses you for one mile, go with him two. If someone takes your cloak, give him also your coat. If someone takes from you what is yours, ask it not back, for indeed you are not able. Give to every one who asks you, and ask it not back; for the Father wills that to all should be given of our own blessings (free gifts). Happy is he who gives according to the commandment, for he is guiltless. Woe to him who receives; for if one receives who has need, he is guiltless; but he who receives not having need shall pay the penalty, why he received and for what. And coming into confinement, he shall be examined concerning the things which he has done, and he shall not escape from there until he pays back the last penny. And also concerning this, it has been said, Let your alms sweat in your hands, until you know to whom you should give.

Chapter 2.

The Second Commandment: Grave Sin Forbidden. And the second commandment of the Teaching; You shall not commit murder, you shall not commit adultery, you shall not commit pederasty (sexual activity involving a man and a boy), you shall not commit fornication, you shall not steal, you shall not practice magic, you shall not practice witchcraft, you shall not murder a child by abortion nor kill that which is born. You shall not covet the things of your neighbor, you shall not swear, you shall not bear false witness, you shall not speak evil, you shall bear no grudge. You shall not be double-minded nor double-tongued, for to be double-tongued is a snare of death. Your speech shall not be false, nor empty, but fulfilled by deed. You shall not be covetous, nor rapacious, nor a hypocrite, nor evil disposed, nor haughty. You shall not take evil counsel against your neighbor. You shall not hate any man; but some you shall reprove, and concerning some you shall pray, and some you shall love more than your own life.

Chapter 3.

237

Other Sins Forbidden. My child, flee from every evil thing, and from every likeness of it. Be not prone to anger, for anger leads to murder. Be neither jealous, nor quarrelsome, nor of hot temper, for out of all these murders are engendered. My child, be not a lustful one. for lust leads to fornication. Be neither a filthy talker, nor of lofty eye, for out of all these adulteries are engendered. My child, be not an observer of omens, since it leads to idolatry. Be neither an enchanter, nor an astrologer, nor a purifier, nor be willing to took at these things, for out of all these idolatry is engendered. My child, be not a liar, since a lie leads to theft. Be neither money-loving, nor vainglorious, for out of all these thefts are engendered. My child, be not a murmurer, since it leads the way to blasphemy. Be neither self-willed nor evil-minded, for out of all these blasphemies are engendered.

Rather, be meek, since the meek shall inherit the earth. Be long-suffering and pitiful and guileless and gentle and good and always trembling at the words which you have heard. You shall not exalt yourself, nor give over-confidence to your soul. Your soul shall not be joined with lofty ones, but with just and lowly ones shall it have its intercourse. Accept whatever happens to you as good, knowing that apart from God nothing comes to pass.

Chapter 4.

Various Precepts. My child, remember night and day him who speaks the word of God to you, and honor him as you do the Lord. For wherever the lordly rule is uttered, there is the Lord. And seek out day by day the faces of the saints, in order that you may rest upon their words. Do not long for division, but rather bring those who contend to peace. Judge righteously, and do not respect persons in reproving for transgressions. You shall not be undecided whether or not it shall be. Be not a stretcher forth of the hands to receive and a drawer of them back to give. If you have anything, through your hands you shall give ransom for your sins. Do not hesitate to give, nor complain when you give; for you shall know who is the good repayer of the hire. Do not turn away from him who is in want; rather, share all things with your brother, and do not say that they are your own. For if you are partakers in that which is immortal, how much more in things which are mortal? Do not remove your hand from your son or daughter; rather, teach them the fear of God from their youth. Do not enjoin anything in your bitterness upon your bondman or maidservant, who hope in the same God, lest ever they shall fear not God who is over both; for he comes not to call according to the outward appearance, but to them whom the Spirit has prepared. And you bondmen shall be subject to your masters as to a type of God, in modesty and fear. You shall hate all hypocrisy and everything which is not pleasing to the Lord. Do not in any way forsake the commandments of the Lord; but keep what you have received, neither adding thereto nor taking away therefrom. In the church you shall acknowledge your transgressions, and you shall not come near for your prayer with an evil conscience. This is the way of life.

Chapter 5.

The Way of Death. And the way of death is this: First of all it is evil and accursed: murders, adultery, lust, fornication, thefts, idolatries, magic arts, witchcrafts, rape, false witness, hypocrisy, double-heartedness, deceit, haughtiness, depravity, self-will, greediness, filthy talking, jealousy, over-confidence, loftiness, boastfulness; persecutors of the good, hating truth, loving a lie, not knowing a reward for righteousness, not cleaving to good nor to righteous judgment, watching not for that which is good, but for that which is evil; from whom meekness and endurance are far, loving vanities, pursuing revenge, not pitying a poor man, not laboring for the afflicted, not knowing Him Who made them, murderers of children, destroyers of the handiwork of God, turning away from him who is in want, afflicting him who is distressed, advocates of the rich, lawless judges of the poor, utter sinners. Be delivered, children, from all these.

Chapter 6.

Against False Teachers, and Food Offered to Idols. See that no one causes you to err from this way of the Teaching, since apart from God it teaches you. For if you are able to bear the entire yoke of the Lord, you will be perfect; but if you are not able to do this, do what you are able. And concerning food, bear what you are able; but against that which is sacrificed to idols be exceedingly careful; for it is the service of dead gods.

Chapter 7.

Concerning Baptism. And concerning baptism, baptize this way:

Having first said all these things, baptize into the name of the Father, and of the Son, and of the Holy Spirit, in living water. But if you have no living water, baptize into other water; and if you cannot do so in cold water, do so in warm. But if you have neither, pour out water three times upon the head into the name of Father and Son and Holy Spirit. But before the baptism let the baptizer fast, and the baptized, and whoever else can; but you shall order the baptized to fast one or two days before.

Chapter 8.

Fasting and Prayer (the Lord's Prayer). But let not your fasts be with the hypocrites, for they fast on the second and fifth day of the week. Rather, fast on the fourth day and the Preparation (Friday). Do not pray like the hypocrites, but rather as the Lord commanded in His Gospel, like this:

Our Father who art in heaven, hallowed be Thy name. Thy kingdom come. Thy will be done on earth, as it is in heaven. Give us today our daily (needful) bread, and forgive us our debt as we also forgive our debtors. And bring us not into temptation, but deliver us from the evil one (or, evil); for Thine is the power and the glory for ever..

Pray this three times each day.

Chapter 9.

The Eucharist. Now concerning the Eucharist, give thanks this way.

First, concerning the cup:

We thank thee, our Father, for the holy vine of David Thy servant, which You madest known to us through Jesus Thy Servant; to Thee be the glory for ever..

And concerning the broken bread:

We thank Thee, our Father, for the life and knowledge which You madest known to us through Jesus Thy Servant; to Thee be the glory for ever. Even as this broken bread was scattered over the hills, and was gathered together and became one, so let Thy Church be gathered together from the ends of the earth into Thy kingdom; for Thine is the glory and the power through Jesus Christ for ever..

But let no one eat or drink of your Eucharist, unless they have been baptized into the name of the Lord; for concerning this also the Lord has said, "Give not that which is holy to the dogs."

Chapter 10.

Prayer after Communion. But after you are filled, give thanks this way:

We thank Thee, holy Father, for Thy holy name which You didst cause to tabernacle in our hearts, and for the knowledge and faith and immortality, which You modest known to us through Jesus Thy Servant; to Thee be the glory for ever. Thou, Master almighty, didst create all things for Thy name's sake; You gavest food and drink to men for enjoyment, that they might give thanks to Thee; but to us You didst freely give spiritual food and drink and life eternal through Thy Servant. Before all things we thank Thee that You are mighty; to Thee be the glory for ever. Remember, Lord, Thy Church, to deliver it from all evil and to make it perfect in Thy love, and gather it from the four winds, sanctified for Thy kingdom which Thou have prepared for it; for Thine is the power and the glory for ever. Let grace come, and let this world pass away. Hosanna to the God (Son) of David! If any one is holy, let him come; if any one is not so, let him repent. Maranatha. Amen.

But permit the prophets to make Thanksgiving as much as they desire.

Chapter 11.

Concerning Teachers, Apostles, and Prophets. Whosoever, therefore, comes and teaches you all these things that have been said before, receive him. But if the teacher himself turns and teaches another doctrine to the destruction of this, hear him not. But if he teaches so as to increase righteousness and the knowledge of the Lord, receive him as the Lord. But concerning the apostles and prophets, act according to the decree of the Gospel. Let every apostle who comes to you be received as the Lord. But he shall not remain more than one day; or two days, if there's a need. But if he remains three days, he is a false prophet. And when the apostle goes away, let him take nothing but bread until he lodges. If he asks for money, he is a false prophet. And every prophet who speaks in the Spirit you shall neither try nor judge; for every sin shall be forgiven, but this sin shall not be forgiven. But not every one who speaks in the Spirit is a prophet; but only if he holds the ways of the Lord. Therefore from their ways shall the false prophet and the prophet be known. And every prophet who orders a meal in the Spirit does not eat it, unless he is indeed a false prophet. And every prophet who teaches the truth, but does not do what he teaches, is a false prophet. And every prophet, proved true, working unto the mystery of the Church in the world, yet not teaching others to do what he himself does, shall not be judged among you, for with God he has his judgment; for so did also the ancient prophets. But whoever says in the Spirit, Give me money, or something else, you shall not listen to him. But if he tells you to give for others' sake who are in need, let no one judge him.

Chapter 12.

Reception of Christians. But receive everyone who comes in the name of the Lord, and prove and know him afterward; for you shall have understanding right and left. If he who comes is a wayfarer, assist him as far as you are able; but he shall not remain with you more than two or three days, if need be. But if he wants to stay with you, and is an artisan, let him work and eat. But if he has no trade, according to your understanding, see to it that, as a Christian, he shall not live with you idle. But if he wills not to do, he is a Christ-monger. Watch that you keep away from such.

Chapter 13.

Support of Prophets. But every true prophet who wants to live among you is worthy of his support. So also a true teacher is himself worthy, as the workman, of his support. Every first-fruit, therefore, of the products of wine-press and threshing-floor, of oxen and of sheep, you shall take and give to the prophets, for they are your high priests. But if you have no prophet, give it to the poor. If you make a batch of dough, take the first-fruit and give according to the commandment. So also when you open a jar of wine or of oil, take the first-fruit and give it to the prophets; and of money (silver) and clothing and every possession, take the first-fruit, as it may seem good to you, and give according to the commandment.

Chapter 14.

Christian Assembly on the Lord's Day. But every Lord's day gather yourselves together, and break bread, and give thanksgiving after having confessed your transgressions, that your sacrifice may be pure. But let no one who is at odds with his fellow come together with you, until they be reconciled, that your sacrifice may not be profaned. For this is that which was spoken by the Lord: "In every place and time offer to me a pure sacrifice; for I am a great King, says the Lord, and my name is wonderful among the nations."

Chapter 15.

Bishops and Deacons; Christian Reproof. Appoint, therefore, for yourselves, bishops and deacons worthy of the Lord, men meek, and not lovers of money, and truthful and proved; for they also render to you the service of prophets and teachers. Therefore do not despise them, for they are your honored ones, together with the prophets and teachers. And reprove one another, not in anger, but in peace, as you have it in the Gospel. But to anyone that acts amiss against another, let no one speak, nor let him hear anything from you until he repents. But your prayers and alms and all your deeds so do, as you have it in the Gospel of our Lord.

Chapter 16.

Watchfulness; the Coming of the Lord. Watch for your life's sake. Let not your lamps be quenched, nor your loins unloosed; but be ready, for you know not the hour in which our Lord will come. But come together often, seeking the things which are befitting to your souls: for the whole time of your faith will not profit you, if you are not made perfect in the last time. For in the last days false prophets and corrupters shall be multiplied, and the sheep shall be turned into wolves, and love shall be turned into hate; for when lawlessness increases, they shall hate and persecute and betray one another, and then shall appear the world-deceiver as Son of God, and shall do signs and wonders, and the earth shall be delivered into his hands, and he shall do iniquitous things which have never yet come to pass since the beginning. Then shall the creation of men come into the fire of trial, and many shall be made to stumble and shall perish; but those who endure in their faith shall be saved from under the curse itself. And then shall appear the signs of the truth: first, the sign of an outspreading in heaven, then the sign of the sound of the trumpet. And third, the resurrection of the dead -- yet not of all, but as it is said: "The Lord shall come and all His saints with Him." Then shall the world see the Lord coming upon the clouds of heaven.

The "Q" Source Based on Luke.

"Q" is an abbreviation for Quelle, the German word for "source." The prevailing theory in the study of the gospels of Matthew, Mark and Luke is that Mark was the first gospel, Matthew and Luke are rewritten versions of Mark. But there are very many sayings in Matthew and in Luke that are NOT in Mark.

These, it is thought, came from a common written source (or Quelle) that is now known as "Q". Often Q sayings are word-for-word the same in Greek in both Matthew and Luke and often are in the same order. This means to most scholars that Q was a written text (no longer in existence) and not simply oral tradition. Many Q sayings are also to be found in the Gospel of Thomas. Thomas is NOT Q but Thomas is a list of saying, like "Q", which in many ways runs parallel to the sayings of "Q".

3:7-9 [John the Baptist] said to the multitudes that came out to be baptized by him, "You brood of vipers! Who warned you to flee from the wrath to come? Bear fruits that befit repentance, and do not begin to say to yourselves, we have Abraham as our father'; for I tell you, God is able from these stones to raise up children to Abraham. Even now the axe is laid to the root of the trees; every tree therefore that does not bear good fruit is cut down and thrown into the fire."

3:16-17 John answered them all, "I baptize you with water; but he who is mightier than I is coming, the thong of whose sandals I am not worthy to untie; he will baptize you with the Holy Spirit and with fire. His winnowing fork is in his hand, to clear his threshing floor, and to gather the wheat into his granary, but the chaff he will burn with unquenchable fire."

4:1-13 Jesus, full of the Holy spirit, returned from the Jordan and was led by the Spirit for forty days in the wilderness, tempted by the devil. He ate nothing in those days; and when they were ended, he was hungry. The devil said to him, "If you are the Son of God, command this stone to become bread." Jesus answered him, "It is written, 'Man shall not live by bread alone." The devil took him up, and showed him all the kingdoms of the world in a moment of time, and said to him, "To you I will give all this authority and their glory; for it has been delivered to me, and I give it to whom I will, if you, then, will worship me, it shall all be yours." And Jesus answered him, 'It is written, 'you shall worship the Lord your God, and him only shall you serve.'" He took him to Jerusalem and set him on the pinnacle of the temple and said to him 'If you are the Son of God throw yourself down from here; for it is written, 'He will give his angels charge of you, to guard you, and on their hands they will bear you up, lest you strike your foot against a stone.' " Jesus answered him, "It is said, 'you shall not tempt the Lord your God.' "And when the devil had ended every temptation, he departed from him until an opportune time.

6:20b-21 Blessed are you poor, for yours is the kingdom of God. Blessed are you that hunger now, for you shall be satisfied. Blessed are you that weep now, for you shall laugh.

6:22-23 Blessed are you when men hate you, and when they exclude you and revile you, and cast out your name as evil, on account of the Son of man! Rejoice in that day, and leap for joy, for behold, your reward is great in heaven; for so their fathers did to the prophets.

6:27-28 But I say to you that hear, Love your enemies, do good to those who hate you, bless those who curse you, pray for those who abuse you.

6:29 To him who strikes you on the cheek, offer the other also; and from him who takes away your cloak do not withhold your coat as well.

6:30 Give to every one who begs from you; and of him who takes away your goods do not ask them again.

6:31 As you wish that men would do to you, do so to them.

6:32-35 If you love those who love you, what credit is that to you? For even sinners love those who love them. If you do good to those who do good to you, what credit is that to you? For even sinners do the same. If you lend to those from whom you hope to receive what credit is that to you? Even sinners lend to sinners, to receive as much again. But love your enemies, and do good, and lend, expecting nothing in return; and your reward will be great, and you will be sons of the Most High; for he is kind to the ungrateful and the selfish.

6:36 Be merciful, even as your Father is merciful.

6:37-38 Judge not, and you will not be judged; condemn not, and you will not be condemned; forgive, and you will be forgiven; and give and it will be given to you; good measure, pressed down, shaken together, running over, will be put into your lap. For the measure you give will be the measure you get back."

6:39 Can a blind man lead a blind man? Will they not both fall into a pit?

6:40 A disciple is not above his teacher, but every one when he is fully taught will be like his teacher.

6:41-42 Why do you see the speck that is in your brother's eye, but do not notice the log that is in your own eye? Or how can you say to your brother, 'Brother, let me take out the speck that is in your eye,' when you yourself do not see the log that is in your own eye? You hypocrite, first take the log out of your own eye, and then you will see clearly to take out the speck that is in your brother's eye.

6:43-44 For no good tree bears bad fruit, nor again does a bad tree bear good fruit; 44 for each tree is known by its own fruit, For figs are not gathered from thorns, nor are grapes picked from a bramble bush.

6:45 The good man out of the good treasure of his heart produces good, and the evil man out of his evil treasure produces evil; for out of the abundance of the heart his mouth speaks.

6:46 Why do you call me 'Lord, Lord,' and not do what I tell you?

6:47-49 Every one who comes to me and hears my words and does them, I will show you what he is like: he is like a man building a house, who dug deep, and built the foundation upon rock; and when a flood arose, the stream broke against that house, and could not shake it, because it had been well built. But he who hears and does not do them is like a man who built a house on the ground without a foundation, against which the stream broke, and immediately it fell, and the ruin of that house was great.

7:1-10 A centurion had a slave who was dear to him who was sick and at the point of death. When he heard of Jesus he sent to him elders of the Jews, asking him to come and heal his slave. When they came to Jesus they besought him earnestly, saying, "He is worthy to have you do this for him, for he loves our nation, and he built us our synagogue." Jesus went with them. When he was not far from the house, the centurion sent friends to him, saying to him, Lord do not trouble yourself, for I am not worthy to have you come under my roof; therefore I did not presume to come to you. But say the word, and let my servant be healed. For I am a man set under authority, with soldiers under me: and I say to one, 'Go,' and he goes; and to another, 'come,' and he comes; and to my slave, 'Do this,' and he does it," when Jesus heard this he marveled at him, and turned and said to the multitude that followed him, 'I tell you, not even in Israel have I found such faith." When those who had been sent returned to the house, they found the slave well.

7:18-23 The disciples of John told him all these things. John calling to him two of his disciples, sent them to the Lord, saying, 'Are you he who is to come, or shall we look or another?" When the men had come to him, they said, John the Baptist has sent us to you, saying, Are you he who is to come or shall we look for another?' In that hour he cured many of diseases and plagues and evil spirits, and on many that were blind he bestowed sight. He answered them, "Go and tell John what you have seen and heard; the blind receive their sight, the lame walk, lepers are cleansed, and the deaf hear, the dead are raised up, the poor have good news preached to them, and blessed is he who takes no offense at me."

7:24-26 When the messengers of John had gone, he began to speak to the crowds concerning John: What did you go out into the wilderness to behold? A reed shaken by the wind? What then did you go out to see? A man clothed in soft raiment? Behold, those who are gorgeously appareled and live in luxury are in kings' courts. What then did you go out to see? A prophet? Yes, I tell you, and more than a prophet.

7:27 This is he of whom it is written, Behold, I send my messenger before thy face, who shall prepare thy way before thee.

7:28 I tell you, among those born of women none is greater than John; yet he who is least in the kingdom of God is greater than he.

7:31-34 To what shall I compare the men of this generation, and what are they like? They are like children sitting in the market place and calling to one another, We piped to you, and you did not dance; we wailed, and you did not weep. John the Baptist has come eating no bread and drinking no wine; and you say, He has a demon.' The Son of man has come eating and drinking; and you say, Behold, a glutton and a drunkard, a friend of tax collectors and sinners!'

7:35 Wisdom is justified by all her children."

9:57-58 Foxes have holes, and birds of the air have nests; but the son of man has nowhere to lay his head.

9:59-60 To another he said, Follow me." But he said, "Lord, let me first go and bury my father." But he said to him, leave the dead to bury their own dead; but as for you, go and proclaim the kingdom of God."

10:2 He said to them, The harvest is plentiful, but the laborers are few; pray therefore the Lord of the harvest to send out laborers into his harvest.

10:3 Go your way; behold, I send you out as lambs in the midst of wolves. Carry no purse, no bag, no sandals; salute no one on the road. Whatever house you enter, first say, 'Peace be to this house!' And if a son of peace is there, your peace shall rest upon him; but if not, it shall return to you.

10:7 Remain in the same house, eating and drinking what they provide, for the laborer deserves his wages. Do not go from house to house.

10:8-9 Whenever you enter a town and they receive you, eat what is set before you; heal the sick in it and say to them, 'The kingdom of God has come near to you.

10:10-11 Whenever you enter a town and they do not receive you, go into its streets and say: 'Even the dust of your town that clings to our feet, we wipe off against you; nevertheless know this, that the kingdom of God has come near.'

10:12 I tell you, it shall be more tolerable on that day for Sodom than for that town.

10:13-15 Woe to you, Chorazin! woe to you, Bethsaida! for if the mighty works done in you had been done in Tyre and Sidon, they would have repented long ago, sitting in sackcloth and ashes. But it shall be more tolerable in the judgement for Tyre and Sidon than for you. And you, Capernaum, will you be exalted to heaven? You shall be brought down to Hades.

10:16 He who hears you hears me, and he who rejects you rejects me, and he who rejects me rejects him who sent me.

10:21-22 He rejoiced in the Holy Spirit and said, 'I thank thee, Father, Lord of heaven and earth, that thou hast hidden these things from the wise and understanding and revealed them to babes; yea, Father, for such was thy gracious will. All things have been delivered to me by my Father; and no one knows who the Son is except the Father, or who the Father is except the Son and any one to whom the Son chooses to reveal him.'

10:23-24 Blessed are the eyes which see what you see! For I tell you that many prophets and kings desired to see what you see, and did not see it, and to hear what you hear, and did not hear it.

11:2-4 When you pray, say, 'Father, hallowed be thy name, Thy kingdom come. Give us each day our daily bread; and forgive us our sins, for we ourselves forgive every one who is indebted to us; and lead us not into temptation.'

11:9-10 Ask, and it will be given you; seek, and you will find; knock, and it will be opened to you. Everyone who asks receives, and he who seeks finds, and to him who knocks it will be opened.

11:11-13 What father among you, if his son asks for a fish, will instead of a fish give him a serpent; 12 or if he asks for an egg, will give him a scorpion? If you then, who are evil, know how to give good gifts to your children, how much more will the heavenly Father give the Holy Spirit to those who ask him!

11:14-15 He was casting out a demon that was dumb; when the demon had gone out, the dumb man spoke, and the people marveled. But some of them said, "He casts out demons by Beelzebub, the prince of demons"

11:17-18 "Every kingdom divided against itself is laid waste, and house falls upon house. If Satan also is divided against himself, how can his kingdom stand?

11:19 For you say that I cast out demons by Beelzebub. If I cast out demons by Beelzebub, by whom do your sons cast them out? Therefore they shall be your judges.

11:20 If it is by the finger of God that I cast out demons, then the kingdom of God has come upon you.

11:21-22 When a strong man, fully armed, guards his own palace, his good are in peace; but when one stronger than he assails him and overcomes him, he takes away his armor in which he trusted and divides his spoil.

11:23 He who is not with me is against me, and he who does not gather with me scatters.

11:24-26 When the unclean spirit has gone out of a man, he passes through waterless places seeking rest; and finding none he says, I will return to my house from which I came.' When he comes he finds it swept and put in order. Then he goes and brings seven spirits more evil than himself, and they enter and dwell there; and the last state of that man becomes worse than the first.

11:29 This generation is an evil generation; it seeks a sign, but no sign shall be given to it except the sign of Jonah.

11:30 As Jonah became a sign to the men of Nineveh, so will the Son of man be to this generation.

11:31-32 The queen of the South will arise at the judgment with the men of this generation and condemn them; for she came from the ends of the earth to hear the wisdom of Solomon, and behold, something greater than Solomon is here. The men of Nineveh will arise at the judgment with this generation and condemn it; for they repented at the preaching of Jonah, and behold, something greater than Jonah is here.

11:33 No one after lighting a lamp puts it in a cellar or under a bush, but on a stand, that those who enter may see the light.

11:34-36 Your eye is the lamp of your body; when your eye is sound, your whole body is full of light; but when it is not sound, your body is full of darkness. Therefore be careful lest the light in you be darkness.

If then your whole body is full of light, having no part dark, it will be wholly bright, as when a lamp with its rays gives you light.

11:39-41 You Pharisees cleanse the outside of the cup and of the dish, but inside you are full of extortion and wickedness. to You fools! Did not he who made the outside make the inside also? But give for alms those things which are within and behold, everything is clean for you.

11:42 Woe to you Pharisees! for you tithe mint and rue and every herb, and neglect justice and the love of God; these you ought to have done, without neglecting the others.

11:43 Woe to you Pharisees! for you love the best seat in the synagogues and salutations in the Market places.

11:44 Woe to you! for you are like graves which are not seen, and men walk over them without knowing it."

11:46 Woe to you lawyers also! for you load men with burdens hard to bear, and you yourselves do not touch the burdens with one of your fingers.

11:47-48 Woe to you for you build the tombs of the prophets whom your fathers killed. So you are witnesses and consent to the deeds of your fathers; they killed them, and you build their tombs. 11:49-51 The Wisdom of God said, "I will send them prophets and apostles, some of whom they will kill and persecute,' that the blood of all the prophets, shed from the foundation of the world may be required of this generation, from the blood of Abel to the blood of Zechariah, who perished between the altar and the sanctuary. Yes, I tell you, it shall be required of this generation.

11:52 Woe to you lawyers! for you have taken away the key of knowledge; you did not enter yourselves and you hindered those who were entering.

12:2 Nothing is covered up that will not be revealed, or hidden that will not be known.

12:3 Whatever you have said in the dark shall be heard in the light, and what you have whispered in private rooms shall be proclaimed upon the housetops.

12:4-5 I tell you, my friends, do not fear those who kill the body, and after that have no more that they can do. But I will warn you whom to fear: fear him who, after he has killed, has power to cast into hell; yes, I tell you fear him!

12:6-7 Are not five sparrows sold for two pennies? And not one of them is forgotten before God. Why even the hairs of your head are all numbered. Fear not; you are of more value than many sparrows.

12:8-9 I tell you, every one who acknowledges me before men, the Son of man also will acknowledge before the angels of God; but he who denies me before men will be denied before the angels of God.

12:10 Every one who speaks a word against the Son of man will be forgiven; but he who blasphemes against the Holy Spirit will not be forgiven.

12:11-12 When they bring you before the synagogues and the rulers and the authorities, do not be anxious how or what you are to answer or what you are to say; for the Holy Spirit will teach you in that very hour what you ought to say.

12:22 Do not be anxious about your life, what you shall eat nor about your body, what you shall put on.

12:23 Life is more than food, and the body more than clothing.

12:24 Consider the ravens, they neither sow nor reap. they have neither storehouse nor barn, and yet God feeds them. Of how much more value are you than the birds !

12:25-26 Which of you by being anxious can add a cubit to his span of life? If then you are not able to do as small a thing as that, why are you anxious about the rest?

12:27 Consider the lilies, how they grow; they neither toil nor spin; yet I tell you, even Solomon in all his glory was not arrayed like one of these.

12:28 But if God so clothes the grass which is alive in the field today and tomorrow is thrown into the oven, how much more will he clothe you, O men of little faith!

12:29-30 Do not seek what you are to eat and what you are to drink, nor be of anxious mind. For all the nations of the world seek these things; and your Father knows that you need them. Instead seek his kingdom, and these things shall be yours as well.

12:33-34 Sell your possessions, and give alms; provide your selves with purses that do not grow old, with a treasure in the heavens that does not fail, where no thief approaches and no moth destroys. For where your treasure is, there will your heart be also.

12:39-40 If the householder had known at what hour the thief was coming, he would have been awake and would not have let his house to be broken into, you also must be ready; for the Son of man is coming at an hour you do not expect.

12:42-46 The Lord said, 'Who then is the faithful and wise steward, whom his master will set over his household, to give them their portion of food at the proper time? Blessed is that servant whom his master when he comes will find so doing. Truly I tell you, he will set him over all his possessions. But if that servant says to himself, 'My master is delayed in coming,' and begins to beat the menservants and the maidservants, and to eat and drink and get drunk, the master of that servant will come on a day when he does not expect him and at an hour he does not know, and will punish him, and put him with the unfaithful.

12:49 I came to cast fire upon the earth; and would that it were already kindled!

12:52-53 Do you think that I have come to give peace on earth? No, I tell you, but rather division; 52 for henceforth in one house there will be five divided, three against two and two against three; they will be divided, father against son and son against father, mother against daughter and daughter against her mother, mother-in-law against her daughter-in-law and daughter-in-law against her mother-in-law.

12:57-59 Why do you not judge for yourselves what is right? As you go with your accuser before the magistrate, make an effort to settle with him on the way, lest he drag you to the judge, and the judge hand you over to the officer, and the officer put you in prison. I tell you, you will never get out till you have paid the very last copper.

13:18-19 He said, "What is the kingdom of God like? To what shall I compare it?' It is like a grain of mustard seed which a man took, and sowed in his garden; and it grew and became a tree, and the birds of the air made nests in its branches."

13:20-21 He said, "To what shall I compare the kingdom of God? 21 It is like leaven which a woman took and hid in three measures of meal, till it was all leavened."

13:24 Strive to enter by the narrow door; for many, I tell you, will seek to enter and will not be able.

13:25-27 When once the householder has risen up and shut the door, you will begin to stand outside and to knock at the door, saying, 'Lord, open to us.' He will answer you, 'I do not know where you come from,' Then you will begin to say, we ate and drank in your presence, and you taught in our streets.' But he will say, 'I tell you, I do not know where you come from; depart from me, all you workers of iniquity!'

13:28-29 You will weep and gnash your teeth, when you see Abraham and Isaac and Jacob and all the prophets in the kingdom of God and you yourselves thrust out. Men will come from east and west, and from north and south, and sit at table in the kingdom of God.

13:30 Some are last who will be first, and some are first who will be last.

13:34-35 0 Jerusalem, Jerusalem! How often would I have gathered your children together as a hen gathers her brood under her wings, and you would not! Behold, your house is forsaken. I tell you, you will not see me until you say, Blessed is he who comes in the name of the Lord!"

14:16-24 A man once gave a great banquet, and invited many and at the time of the banquet he sent his servant to say to those who had been invited, 'Come for all is now ready.' But they all alike began to make excuses. The first said to him, 'I have bought a field, and I must go out and see it; I pray you, have me excused.' 19 And another said, 'I have bought a yoke of oxen, I pray you, have me excused,' And another said, 'I have married a wife, and therefore I cannot come.' So the servant came and reported this to his master. Then the householder in anger said to his servant, Go out quickly to the streets and lanes of the city, and bring in the poor and maimed and blind and lame,' And the servant said, 'Sir, what you commanded has been done, and still there is room. The master said to the servant, 'Go out to the highways and hedges, and compel people to come in, that my house may be filled. For I tell you, none of those men who were invited shall taste my banquet.'

14:25-26 If any one comes to me and does not hate his own father and mother and wife and children and brothers and sisters, yes, and even his own life, he cannot be my disciple.

14:27 Whoever does not bear his own cross and come after me, cannot be my disciple.

14:34-35 Salt is good; but if salt has lost its taste, how shall its saltiness be restored? It is fit neither for the land nor for the dunghill; men throw it away. He who has ears to hear, let him hear.

15:3-7 What man among you, having a hundred sheep, if he has lost one of them, does not leave the ninety-nine in the wilderness, and go after the one which is lost, until he finds it? And when he has found it, he lays it on his shoulders, rejoicing. When he comes home, he calls together his friends and his neighbors, saying to them, 'Rejoice with me, for I have found my sheep which was lost.' Just so, I tell you, there will be more joy in heaven over one sinner who repents than over ninety-nine righteous persons who need no repentance.'

16:13 No servant can serve two masters; for either he will hate the one and love the other, or he will be devoted to the one and despise the other. You cannot serve God and mammon.

16:16 The law and the prophets were until John; since then the good news of the kingdom of God is preached, and every one enters it violently.

16:17 It is easier for heaven and earth to pass away, than for one dot of the law to become void.

16:18 Every one who divorces his wife and marries another commits adultery, and he who marries a woman divorced from her husband commits adultery.

17:1-2 Temptations to sin are sure to come; but woe to him by whom they come! It would be better for him if a millstone were hung round his neck and he were cast into the sea, than that he should cause one of these little ones to sin.

17:3-4 If your brother sins, rebuke him, and if he repents, forgive him; and if he sins against you seven times in the day, and turns to you seven times, and says, 'I repent,' you must forgive him.

17:5-6 The apostles said to the Lord, "Increase our faith!" The Lord said, "If you had faith as a grain of mustard seed, you could say to this mulberry tree, 'Be rooted up, and be planted in the sea,' and it would obey you."

17:23 They will say to you, 'Lo, there!' or 'Lo, here!' Do not go, do not follow them.

17:24 As the lightning lights up the sky from one side to the other, so will Son of man be in his day.

17:26-27 As it was in the days of Noah, so will it be in the days of the Son of man. They ate, they drank, they married, they were given in marriage, until the day when Noah entered the ark, and the flood came and destroyed then all.

17:28-30 As it was in the days of Lot; they ate, they drank, they bought, they sold, they planted, they built, but on the day when Lot went out from Sodom fire and brimstone rained from heaven and destroyed them all. So will it be on the day when the Son of man is revealed.

17:33 Whoever seeks to gain his life will lose it, but whoever loses his life will preserve it.

17:34-35 I tell you, in that night there will be two men in one bed; one will be taken and the other left. There will be two women grinding together; one will be taken and the other left.

17:37 They said to him, "Where Lord?" He said to them, "Where the corpse is, there the eagles will be gathered together."

19:12-24 He said to them, "A nobleman went into a far country to receive kingly power and then return. Calling ten of his servants, he gave them ten pounds, and said to them, 'Trade with these till I come.' But his citizens hated him and sent an embassy after him, saying, 'We do not want this man to reign over us.' When he returned, having received the kingly power, he commanded these servants to whom he had given the money, to be called to him, that he might know what they had gained by trading. The first came before him saying 'Lord, your pound has made ten pounds more.' And he said to him, 'Well done, good servant! Because you have been faithful in a very little, you shall have authority over ten cities.' The second came, saying, 'Lord, your pound has made five pounds,' He said to him; 'And you are to be over five cities.' Then another came, saying, 'Lord here is your pound, which I kept laid away in a napkin; for I was afraid of you, because you are a severe man; you take up what you did not lay down, and reap what you did not sow.' He said to him, 'I will condemn you out of your own mouth, you wicked servant! You knew that I was a severe man, taking up what I did not lay down and reaping what I did not sow? Why then did you not put my money into the bank, and at my coming I should have collected it with interest?'

He said to those who stood by, 'Take the pound from him, and give it to him who has ten pounds.' They said to him, 'Lord, he has ten pounds!'

19:25-27 I tell you, that to every one who has more will be given; but from him who has not, even what he has will be taken away.

22:28-30 You are those who have continued with me in my trials; as my Father appointed a kingdom for me, so do I appoint for you that you may eat and drink at my table in my kingdom, and sit on thrones judging the twelve tribes of Israel.

Gospel of Thomas
History and Introduction

In the winter of 1945, in Upper Egypt, an Arab peasant was gathering fertilizer and topsoil for his crops. While digging in the soft dirt he came across a large earthen vessel. Inside were scrolls containing hitherto unseen books.

The scrolls were discovered near the site of the ancient town of Chenoboskion, at the base of a mountain named Gebel et-Tarif, near Hamra-Dum, in the vicinity of Naj 'Hammadi, about sixty miles from Luxor in Egypt. The texts were written in the Coptic language and preserved on papyrus sheets. The lettering style dated them as having been penned around the third or fourth century A.D. The Gospel of Thomas is the longest of the volumes consisting of between 114 and 118 verses. Recent study indicates that the original works, of which the scrolls are copies, may predate the four canonical gospels of Matthew, Mark, Luke, and John. The origin of The Gospel of Thomas is now thought to be from the first or second century A.D.

The peasant boy who found this treasure stood to be rewarded greatly. This could have been the discovery of a lifetime for his family, but the boy had no idea what he had. He took the scrolls home, where his mother burned some as kindling. Others were sold to the black market antique dealers in Cairo. It would be years until they found their way into the hands of a scholar. Part of the thirteenth codex was smuggled from Egypt to America. In 1955 the existence of the codex had reached the ears of Gilles Quispel, a professor of religion and history in the Netherlands. The race was on to find and translate the scrolls.

The introduction of the collected sayings of Jesus refers to the writer as "Didymus (Jude) Thomas." This is the same Thomas who doubted Jesus and was then told to place his hand within the breach in the side of the Savior. In the Gospel of St. John, he is referred to as "Didymus," which means "twin" in Greek. In Aramaic, the name "Jude" (or Judas) also carries the sense of "twin". The use of this title led some in the apocryphal tradition to believe that he was the brother and confidant of Jesus. However, when applied to Jesus himself, the literal meaning of "twin" must be rejected by orthodox Christianity as well as anyone adhering to the doctrine of the virgin birth of the only begotten son of God. The title is likely meant to signify that Thomas was a close confidant of Jesus.

Ancient church historians mention that Thomas preached to the Parthians in Persia and it is said he was buried in Edessa.

Fourth century chronicles attribute the evangelization of India (Asia-Minor or Central Asia) to Thomas.

The texts, which some believe predate the four gospels, has a very Zen-like or Eastern flavor. Since it is widely held that the four gospels of Matthew, Mark, Luke, and John have a common reference in the basic text of Mark, it stands to reason that all follow the same general insight and language. Since scholars believe that the Gospel of Thomas predates the four main gospels, it can be assumed it was written outside the influences common to the other gospels. Although the codex found in Egypt is dated to the fourth century, the actual construction of the text of Thomas is placed by most Biblical scholars at about 70 – 150 A.D.

If Thomas wrote his gospel first, without input from Mark, and from the standpoint of Eastern exposure as a result of his sojourn into India, it could explain the "Eastern" quality of the text.

Moreover, there is some speculation that the sayings found in Thomas could be more accurate to the original intent and wording of Jesus than the other gospels. This may seem counter-intuitive until we realize that Christianity itself is an Eastern religion, albeit Middle-Eastern. Although, as it spread west the faith went through many changes to westernize or Romanize it...Jesus was both mystical and Middle-Eastern.

The Gospel of Thomas was most likely composed in Syria, where tradition holds the church of Edessa was founded by Judas Thomas, "The Twin" (Didymos). The gospel may well be the earliest written tradition in the Syriac church

The Gospel of Thomas is sometimes called a Gnostic gospel. The term "Gnostic" derives from "gnosis," which in Greek means "knowledge." Gnostics believed that knowledge is formed or found from a personal encounter with God brought about by inward or intuitive insight. They believed they were privy to a secret knowledge about the divine. It is this knowledge that leads to their name. It is possible that the roots of the Gnostic system pre-dates Christianity and found a suitable home in the mystical side of the Christian faith.

There are numerous references to the Gnostics in second century literature. Their form of Christianity was considered heresy by the early church fathers. It is from the writings condemning the group that we glean most of our information. They are alluded to in the Bible in 1 Tm 1:4 and 1 Tm 6:20, and possibly the entirety of Jude, as the writers of the Bible defended their theology against that of the Gnostics.

Gospel of Thomas

These are the secret sayings which the living Jesus has spoken and Judas who is also Thomas (the twin) (Didymos Judas Thomas) wrote.

1. And he said: Whoever finds the interpretation of these sayings will not taste death.

2. Jesus said: Let he who seeks not stop seeking until he finds, and when he finds he will be troubled, and when he has been troubled he will marvel (be astonished) and he will reign over all and in reigning, he will find rest.

3. Jesus said: If those who lead you said to you: Behold, the Kingdom is in the sky, then the birds of the sky would enter before you. If they said to you: It is in the sea, then the fish of the sea would enter ahead you. But the Kingdom of God exists within you and it exists outside of you. Those who come to know (recognize) themselves will find it, and when you come to know yourselves you will become known and you will realize that you are the children of the Living Father. Yet if you do not come to know yourselves then you will dwell in poverty and it will be you who are that poverty.

4. Jesus said: The person of old age will not hesitate to ask a little

child of seven days about the place of life, and he will live. For many who are first will become last, (and the last will be first). And they will become one and the same.

5. Jesus said: Recognize what is in front of your face, and what has been hidden from you will be revealed to you. For there is nothing hidden which will not be revealed (become manifest), and nothing buried that will not be raised.

6. His Disciples asked Him, how do you want us to fast, and how will we pray? And how will we be charitable (give alms), and what laws of diet will we maintain?

Jesus said: Do not lie, and do not practice what you hate, for everything is in the plain sight of Heaven. For there is nothing concealed that will not become manifest, and there is nothing covered that will not be exposed.

7. Jesus said: Blessed is the lion that the man will eat, for the lion will become the man. Cursed is the man that the lion shall eat, and still the lion will become man.

8. And he said: The Kingdom of Heaven is like a wise fisherman who casts his net into the sea. He drew it up from the sea full of small fish. Among them he found a fine large fish. That wise fisherman threw all the small fish back into the sea and chose the large fish without

hesitation. Whoever has ears to hear, let him hear!

9. Jesus said: Now, the sower came forth. He filled his hand and threw (the seeds). Some fell upon the road and the birds came and gathered them up. Others fell on the stone and they did not take deep enough roots in the soil, and so did not produce grain. Others fell among the thorns and they choked the seed, and the worm ate them. Others fell upon the good earth and it produced good fruit up toward the sky, it bore 60 fold and 120 fold.

10. Jesus said: I have cast fire upon the world and behold, I guard it until it is ablaze.

11. Jesus said: This sky will pass away, and the one above it will pass away. The dead are not alive, and the living will not die. In the days when you consumed what is dead, you made it alive. When you come into the Light, what will you do? On the day when you were united (one), you became separated (two). When you have become separated (two), what will you do?

12. The Disciples said to Jesus: We know that you will go away from us. Who is it that will be our teacher?

Jesus said to them: Wherever you are (in the place that you have come), you will go to James the Righteous, for whose sake Heaven and Earth were made (came into being).

13. Jesus said to his Disciples: Compare me to others, and tell me who I am like. Simon Peter said to him: You are like a righteous messenger (angel) of God. Matthew said to him: You are like a (wise) philosopher (of the heart). Thomas said to him: Teacher, my mouth is not capable of saying who you are like!

Jesus said: I'm not your teacher, now that you have drunk; you have become drunk from the bubbling spring that I have tended (measured out). And he took him, and withdrew and spoke three words to him: "ahyh ashr ahyh" (I am Who I am).

Now when Thomas returned to his comrades, they inquired of him: What did Jesus said to you? Thomas said to them: If I tell you even one of the words which he spoke to me, you will take up stones and throw them at me, and fire will come from the stones to consume you.

14. Jesus said to them: If you fast, you will give rise to transgression (sin) for yourselves. And if you pray, you will be condemned. And if you give alms, you will cause harm (evil) to your spirits. And when you go into the countryside, if they take you in (receive you) then eat what they set before you and heal the sick among them. For what goes into your mouth will not defile you, but rather what comes out of your mouth, that is what will defile you.

15. Jesus said: When you see him who was not born of woman, bow yourselves down upon your faces and worship him for he is your Father.

16. Jesus said: People think perhaps I have come to spread peace upon the world. They do not know that I have come to cast dissention (conflict) upon the earth; fire, sword, war. For there will be five in a house. Three will be against two and two against three, the father against the son and the son against the father. And they will stand alone.

17. Jesus said: I will give to you what eye has not seen, what ear has not heard, what hand has not touched, and what has not occurred to the mind of man.

18. The Disciples said to Jesus: Tell us how our end will come. Jesus said: Have you already discovered the beginning (origin), so that you inquire about the end? Where the beginning (origin) is, there the end will be. Blessed be he who will take his place in the beginning (stand at the origin) for he will know the end, and he will not experience death.

19. Jesus said: Blessed is he who came into being before he came into being. If you become my Disciples and heed my sayings, these stones will serve you. For there are five trees in paradise for you, which are undisturbed in summer and in winter and their leaves do

not fall. Whoever knows them will not experience death.

20. The Disciples said to Jesus: Tell us what the Kingdom of Heaven is like. He said to them: It is like a mustard seed, smaller than all other seeds and yet when it falls on the tilled earth, it produces a great plant and becomes shelter for the birds of the sky.

21. Mary said to Jesus: Who are your Disciples like? He said: They are like little children who are living in a field that is not theirs. When the owners of the field come, they will say: Let us have our field! It is as if they were naked in front of them (They undress in front of them in order to let them have what is theirs) and they give back the field. Therefore I said, if the owner of the house knows that the thief is coming, he will be alert before he arrives and will not allow him to dig through into the house to carry away his belongings. You, must be on guard and beware of the world (system). Prepare yourself (arm yourself) with great strength or the bandits will find a way to reach you, for the problems you expect will come. Let there be among you a person of understanding (awareness). When the crop ripened, he came quickly with his sickle in his hand to reap. Whoever has ears to hear, let him hear!

22. Jesus saw little children who were being suckled. He said to his Disciples: These little children who are being suckled are like those who enter the Kingdom.

They said to him: Should we become like little children in order to enter the Kingdom?

Jesus said to them: When you make the two one, and you make the inside as the outside and the outside as the inside, when you make the above as the below, and if you make the male and the female one and the same (united male and female) so that the man will not be masculine (male) and the female be not feminine (female), when you establish an eye in the place of an eye and a hand in the place of a hand and a foot in the place of a foot and an likeness (image) in the place of a likeness (an image), then will you enter the Kingdom.

23. Jesus said: I will choose you, one out of a thousand and two out of ten thousand and they will stand as a single one.

24. His Disciples said: Show us the place where you are (your place), for it is necessary for us to seek it.

He said to them: Whoever has ears, let him hear! Within a man of light there is light, and he illumines the entire world. If he does not shine, he is darkness (there is darkness).

25. Jesus said: Love your friend (Brother) as your soul; protect him as you would the pupil of your own eye.

26. Jesus said: You see the speck in your brother's eye but the beam

that is in your own eye you do not see. When you remove the beam out of your own eye, then will you see clearly to remove the speck out of your brother's eye.

27. Jesus said: Unless you fast from the world (system), you will not find the Kingdom of God. Unless you keep the Sabbath (entire week) as Sabbath, you will not see the Father.

28. Jesus said: I stood in the midst of the world. In the flesh I appeared to them. I found them all drunk; I found none thirsty among them. My soul grieved for the sons of men, for they are blind in their hearts and do not see that they came into the world empty they are destined (determined) to leave the world empty. However, now they are drunk. When they have shaken off their wine, then they will repent (change their ways).

29. Jesus said: If the flesh came into being because of spirit, it is a marvel, but if spirit came into being because of the body, it would be a marvel of marvels. I marvel indeed at how great wealth has taken up residence in this poverty.

30. Jesus said: Where there are three gods, they are gods (Where there are three gods they are without god). Where there is only one, I say that I am with him. Lift the stone and there you will find me, Split the wood and there am I.

31. Jesus said: No prophet is accepted in his own village, no physician heals those who know him.

32. Jesus said: A city being built (and established) upon a high mountain and fortified cannot fall nor can it be hidden.

33. Jesus said: What you will hear in your ear preach from your rooftops. For no one lights a lamp and sets it under a basket nor puts it in a hidden place, but rather it is placed up a lamp-stand so that everyone who comes and goes will see its light.

34. Jesus said: If a blind person leads a blind person, both fall into a pit.

35. Jesus said: It is impossible for anyone to enter the house of a strong man to take it by force unless he binds his hands, then he will be able to loot his house.

36. Jesus said: Do not worry from morning to evening nor from evening to morning about the food that you will eat nor about what clothes you will wear. You are much superior to the Lilies which neither card nor spin. When you have no clothing, what do you wear? Who can add time to your life (increase your stature)? He himself will give to you your garment.

37. His Disciples said: When will you appear to us, and when will we

see you?

Jesus said: When you take off your garments without being ashamed, and place your garments under your feet and tread on them as the little children do, then will you see the Son of the Living-One, and you will not be afraid.

38. Jesus said: Many times have you yearned to hear these sayings which I speak to you, and you have no one else from whom to hear them. There will be days when you will seek me but you will not find me.

39. Jesus said: The Pharisees and the Scribes have received the keys of knowledge, but they have hidden them. They did not go in, nor did they permit those who wished to enter to do so. However, you be as wise (astute) as serpents and innocent as doves.

40. Jesus said: A grapevine has been planted outside the (vineyard of the) Father, and since it is not viable (supported) it will be pulled up by its roots and destroyed.

41. Jesus said: Whoever has (it) in his hand, to him will (more) be given. And whoever does not have, from him will be taken even the small amount which he has.

42. Jesus said: Become passers-by.

43. His Disciples said to him: Who are you, that you said these things to us?

Jesus said to them: You do not recognize who I am from what I said to you, but rather you have become like the Jews who either love the tree and hate its fruit, or love the fruit and hate the tree.

44. Jesus said: Whoever blasphemes against the Father, it will be forgiven him. And whoever blasphemes against the Son, it will be forgiven him. Yet whoever blasphemes against the Holy Spirit, it will not be forgiven him neither on earth nor in heaven.

45. Jesus said: Grapes are not harvested from thorns, nor are figs gathered from thistles, for they do not give fruit. A good person brings forth goodness out of his storehouse. A bad person brings forth evil out of his evil storehouse which is in his heart, and he speaks evil, for out of the abundance of the heart he brings forth evil.

46. Jesus said: From Adam until John the Baptist there is none born of women who surpasses John the Baptist, so that his eyes should not be downcast (lowered). Yet I have said that whoever among you becomes like a child will know the Kingdom, and he will be greater than John.

47. Jesus said: It is impossible for a man to mount two horses or to draw two bows, and a servant cannot serve two masters, otherwise he will honor the one and disrespect the other. No man drinks vintage wine and immediately desires to drink new wine, and they do not put new wine into old wineskins or they would burst, and they do not put vintage wine into new wineskins or it would spoil (sour). They do not sew an old patch on a new garment because that would cause a split.

48. Jesus said: If two make peace with each other in this one house, they will say to the mountain: Be moved! and it will be moved.

49. Jesus said: Blessed is the solitary and chosen, for you will find the Kingdom. You have come from it, and unto it you will return.

50.   Jesus said: If they said to you: From where do you come? Say to them: We have come from the Light, the place where the Light came into existence of its own accord and he stood and appeared in their image. If they said to you: Is it you? (Who are you?), say: We are his Sons and we are the chosen of the Living Father. If they ask you: What is the sign of your Father in you? Say to them: It is movement with rest.

51. His Disciples said to him: When will the rest of the dead occur, and when will the New World come? He said to them: That which you look for has already come, but you do not recognize it.

52. His Disciples said to him: Twenty-four prophets preached in Israel, and they all spoke of (in) you. He said to them: You have ignored the Living-One who is in your presence and you have spoken only of the dead.

53. His Disciples said to him: Is circumcision beneficial or not? He said to them: If it were beneficial, their father would beget them already circumcised from their mother. However, the true spiritual circumcision has become entirely beneficial.

54. Jesus said: Blessed be the poor, for yours is the Kingdom of the Heaven.

55. Jesus said: Whoever does not hate his father and his mother will not be able to become my Disciple. And whoever does not hate his brothers and his sisters and does not take up his own cross in my way, will not become worthy of me.

56. Jesus said: Whoever has come to understand the world (system) has found a corpse, and whoever has found a corpse, is superior to the world (of him the system is not worthy).

57. Jesus said: The Kingdom of the Father is like a person who has good seed. His enemy came by night and sowed a weed among the good seed. The man did not permit them to pull up the weed, he said

to them: perhaps you will intend to pull up the weed and you pull up the wheat along with it. But, on the day of harvest the weeds will be very visible and then they will pull them and burn them.

58. Jesus said: Blessed is the person who has suffered, for he has found life. (Blessed is he who has suffered [to find life] and found life).

59. Jesus said: Look to the Living-One while you are alive, otherwise, you might die and seek to see him and will be unable to find him.

60. They saw a Samaritan carrying a lamb, on his way to Judea. Jesus said to them: Why does he take the lamb with him? They said to him: So that he may kill it and eat it. He said to them: While it is alive he will not eat it, but only after he kills it and it becomes a corpse. They said: How could he do otherwise? He said to them: Look for a place of rest for yourselves, otherwise, you might become corpses and be eaten.

61. Jesus said: Two will rest on a bed and one will die and the other will live. Salome said: Who are you, man? As if sent by someone, you laid upon my bed and you ate from my table. Jesus said to her: "I-Am" he who is from that which is whole (the undivided). I have been given the things of my Father. Salome said: I'm your Disciple.

Jesus said to her: Thus, I said that whenever someone is one (undivided)

he will be filled with light, yet whenever he is divided (chooses) he will be filled with darkness.

62. Jesus said: I tell my mysteries to those who are worthy of my mysteries. Do not let your right hand know what your left hand is doing.

63. Jesus said: There was a wealthy person who had much money, and he said: I will use my money so that I may sow and reap and replant, to fill my storehouses with grain so that I lack nothing. This was his intention (is what he thought in his heart) but that same night he died. Whoever has ears, let him hear!

64. Jesus said: A person had houseguests, and when he had prepared the banquet in their honor he sent his servant to invite the guests. He went to the first, he said to him: My master invites you. He replied: I have to do business with some merchants. They are coming to see me this evening. I will go to place my orders with them. I ask to be excused from the banquet. He went to another, he said to him: My master has invited you. He replied to him: I have just bought a house and they require me for a day. I will have no spare time. He came to another, he said to him: My master invites you. He replied to him: My friend is getting married and I must arrange a banquet for him. I will not be able to come. I ask to be excused from the banquet. He went to

another, he said to him: My master invites you. He replied to him: I have bought a farm. I go to receive the rent. I will not be able to come. I ask to be excused. The servant returned, he said to his master: Those whom you have invited to the banquet have excused themselves. The master said to his servant: Go out to the roads, bring those whom you find so that they may feast. And he said: Businessmen and merchants will not enter the places of my Father.

65. He said: A kind person who owned a vineyard leased it to tenants so that they would work it and he would receive the fruit from them. He sent his servant so that the tenants would give to him the fruit of the vineyard. They seized his servant and beat him nearly to death. The servant went, he told his master what had happened. His master said: Perhaps they did not recognize him. So, he sent another servant. The tenants beat him also. Then the owner sent his son. He said: Perhaps they will respect my son. Since the tenants knew that he was the heir to the vineyard, they seized him and killed him. Whoever has ears, let him hear!

66. Jesus said: Show me the stone which the builders have rejected. It is that one that is the cornerstone (keystone).

67. Jesus said: Those who know everything but themselves, lack everything. (whoever knows the all and still feels a personal lacking, he is completely deficient).

68. Jesus said: Blessed are you when you are hated and persecuted, but they themselves will find no reason why you have been persecuted.

69. Jesus said: Blessed are those who have been persecuted in their heart these are they who have come to know the Father in truth. Jesus said: Blessed are the hungry, for the stomach of him who desires to be filled will be filled.

70. Jesus said: If you bring forth what is within you, it will save you. If you do not have it within you to bring forth, that which you lack will destroy you.

71. Jesus said: I will destroy this house, and no one will be able to build it again.

72. A person said to him: Tell my brothers to divide the possessions of my father with me. He said to him: Oh man, who made me a divider? He turned to his Disciples, he said to them: I'm not a divider, am I?

73. Jesus said: The harvest is indeed plentiful, but the workers are few. Ask the Lord to send workers for the harvest.

74. He said: Lord, there are many around the well, yet there is nothing in the well. How is it that many are around the well and no

one goes into it?

75. Jesus said: There are many standing at the door, but only those who are alone are the ones who will enter into the Bridal Chamber.

76. Jesus said: The Kingdom of the Father is like a rich merchant who found a pearl. The merchant was prudent. He sold his fortune and bought the one pearl for himself. You also, seek for his treasure which does not fail, which endures where no moth can come near to eat it nor worm to devour it.

77. Jesus said: "I-Am" the Light who is over all things, "I-Am" the All. From me all came forth and to me all return (The All came from me and the All has come to me). Split wood, there am I. Lift up the stone and there you will find me.

78. Jesus said: Why did you come out to the wilderness; to see a reed shaken by the wind? And to see a person dressed in fine (soft – plush) garments like your rulers and your dignitaries? They are clothed in plush garments, and they are not able to recognize (understand) the truth.

79. A woman from the multitude said to him: Blessed is the womb which bore you, and the breasts which nursed you! He said to her: Blessed are those who have heard the word (meaning) of the Father and have truly kept it. For there will be days when you will say:

Blessed be the womb which has not conceived and the breasts which have not nursed.

80. Jesus said: Whoever has come to understand (recognize) the world (world system) has found a corpse, and whoever has found the corpse, of him the world (world system) is not worthy.

81. Jesus said: Whoever has become rich should reign, and let whoever has power renounce it.

82. Jesus said: Whoever is close to me is close to the fire, and whoever is far from me is far from the Kingdom.

83. Jesus said: Images are visible to man but the light which is within them is hidden. The light of the father will be revealed, but he (his image) is hidden in the light.

84. Jesus said: When you see your reflection, you rejoice. Yet when you perceive your images which have come into being before you, which neither die nor can be seen, how much will you have to bear?

85. Jesus said: Adam came into existence from a great power and a great wealth, and yet he was not worthy of you. For if he had been worthy, he would not have tasted death.

86. Jesus said: The foxes have their dens and the birds have their

nests, yet the Son of Man has no place to lay his head for rest.

87. Jesus said: Wretched is the body which depends upon another body, and wretched is the soul which depends on these two (upon their being together).

88. Jesus said: The angels and the prophets will come to you, and what they will give you belongs to you. And you will give them what you have, and said among yourselves: When will they come to take (receive) what belongs to them?

89. Jesus said: Why do you wash the outside of your cup? Do you not understand (mind) that He who creates the inside is also He who creates the outside?

90. Jesus said: Come unto me, for my yoke is comfortable (natural) and my lordship is gentle— and you will find rest for yourselves.

91. They said to him: Tell us who you are, so that we may believe in you. He said to them: You examine the face of the sky and of the earth, yet you do not recognize Him who is here with you, and you do not know how to seek in (to inquire of Him at) this moment (you do not know how to take advantage of this opportunity).

92. Jesus said: Seek and you will find. But in the past I did not answer the questions you asked. Now I wish to tell them to you, but

you do not ask about (no longer seek) them.

93. Jesus said: Do not give what is sacred to the dogs, lest they throw it on the dung heap. Do not cast the pearls to the swine, lest they cause it to become dung (mud).

94. Jesus said: Whoever seeks will find. And whoever knocks, it will be opened to him.

95. Jesus said: If you have money, do not lend at interest, but rather give it to those from whom you will not be repaid.

96. Jesus said: The Kingdom of the Father is like a woman who has taken a little yeast and hidden it in dough. She produced large loaves of it. Whoever has ears, let him hear!

97. Jesus said: The Kingdom of the Father is like a woman who was carrying a jar full of grain. While she was walking on a road far from home, the handle of the jar broke and the grain poured out behind her onto the road. She did not know it. She had noticed no problem. When she arrived in her house, she set the jar down and found it empty.

98. Jesus said: The Kingdom of the Father is like someone who wished to slay a prominent person. While still in his own house he drew his sword and thrust it into the wall in order to test whether his

hand would be strong enough. Then he slew the prominent person.

99. His Disciples said to him: Your brethren and your mother are standing outside. He said to them: Those here who do my Father's desires are my Brethren and my Mother. It is they who will enter the Kingdom of my Father.

100. They showed Jesus a gold coin, and said to him: The agents of Caesar extort taxes from us. He said to them: Give the things of Caesar to Caesar, give the things of God to God, and give to me what is mine.

101. Jesus said: Whoever does not hate his father and his mother as I do, will not be able to become my Disciple. And whoever does not love his Father and his Mother as I do, will not be able to become my Disciple. For my mother bore me, yet my true Mother gave me the life.

102. Jesus said: Damn these Pharisees. They are like a dog sleeping in the feed trough of oxen. For neither does he eat, nor does he allow the oxen to eat.

103. Jesus said: Blessed is the person who knows at what place of the house the bandits may break in, so that he can rise and collect his things and prepare himself before they enter.

104. They said to him: Come, let us pray today and let us fast. Jesus said: What sin have I committed? How have I been overcome (undone)? When the Bridegroom comes forth from the Bridal Chamber, then let them fast and let them pray.

105. Jesus said: Whoever acknowledges (comes to know) father and mother, will be called the son of a whore.

106. Jesus said: When you make the two one, you will become Sons of Man (children of Adam), and when you say to the mountain: Move! It will move.

107. Jesus said: The Kingdom is like a shepherd who has a hundred sheep. The largest one of them went astray. He left the ninety-nine and sought for the one until he found it. Having searched until he was weary, he said to that sheep: I desire you more than the ninety-nine.

108. Jesus said: Whoever drinks from my mouth will become like me. I will become him, and the secrets will be revealed to him.

109. Jesus said: The Kingdom is like a person who had a treasure hidden in his field and knew nothing of it. After he died, he bequeathed it to his son. The son accepted the field knowing nothing of the treasure. He sold it. Then the person who bought it came and plowed it. He found the treasure. He began to lend money at interest to whomever he wished.

110. Jesus said: Whoever has found the world (system) and becomes wealthy (enriched by it), let him renounce the world (system).

111. Jesus said: Heaven and earth will roll up before you, but he who lives within the Living-One will neither see nor fear death. For, Jesus said: Whoever finds himself, of him the world is not worthy.

112. Jesus said: Damned is the flesh which depends upon the soul. Damned is the soul which depends upon the flesh.

113. His Disciples said to him: When will the Kingdom come? Jesus said: It will not come by expectation (because you watch or wait for it). They will not say: Look here! or: Look there! But the Kingdom of the Father is spread upon the earth, and people do not realize it.

114. Simon Peter said to them: Send Mary away from us, for women are not worthy of this life. Jesus said: Behold, I will draw her into me so that I make her male, in order that she herself will become a living spirit like you males. For every female who becomes male will enter the Kingdom of the Heavens.

Joseph Lumpkin

Made in the USA
Monee, IL
01 April 2021